To Kim:
With thanks for your friendship,

Ed

The Gathering Crisis in Federal Deposit Insurance

MIT Press Series on the Regulation of Economic Activity

General Editor
Richard Schmalensee, MIT Sloan School of Management

1. *Freight Transport Regulation*, Ann F. Friedlaender and Richard H. Spady, 1981
2. *The SEC and the Public Interest*, Susan M. Phillips and J. Richard Zecher, 1981
3. *The Economics and Politics of Oil Price Regulation*, Joseph P. Kalt, 1981
4. *Studies in Public Regulation*, Gray Fromm, editor, 1981
5. *Incentives for Environmental Protection*, Thomas C. Schelling, editor, 1983
6. *United States Oil Pipeline Markets: Structure, Pricing, and Public Policy*, John A. Hansen, 1983
7. *Folded, Spindled, and Mutilated: Economic Analysis and U.S. v. IBM*, Franklin M. Fisher, John J. McGowan, and Joen E. Greenwood, 1983
8. *Targeting Economic Incentives for Environmental Protection*, Albert L. Nichols, 1984
9. *Deregulation and the New Airline Entrepreneurs*, John R. Meyer and Clinton V. Oster, Jr., with Marni Clippinger, Andrew McKey, Don H. Pickrell, John Strong, and C. Kurt Zorn, 1984
10. *Deregulating the Airlines*, Elizabeth E. Bailey, David R. Graham, and Daniel P. Kaplan, 1985
11. *The Gathering Crisis in Federal Deposit Insurance*, Edward J. Kane, 1985

The Gathering Crisis in Federal Deposit Insurance

Edward J. Kane

The MIT Press
Cambridge, Massachusetts
London, England

© 1985 by The Massachusetts Institute of Technology

All rights reserved. No part of this book may be reproduced in any form by any electronic or mechanical means (including photocopying, recording, or information storage and retrieval) without permission in writing from the publisher.

This book was set in Times Roman
by The MIT Press Computergraphics Department
and printed and bound by Halliday Lithograph
in the United States of America.

Library of Congress Cataloging in Publication Data

Kane, Edward J.
 The gathering crisis in Federal Deposit Insurance.

 (MIT Press series on the regulation of economic activity; 11)
 Includes bibliographies and index.
 1. Banks and banking—United States—Government guaranty of deposits. I. Title.
II. Series.
HG1662.U5K36 1985   332.1'0973   85-6629
ISBN 0-262-11102-0

To my parents

Contents

Series Foreword	ix
Acknowledgments	xi

Chapter 1
Why Federal Deposit Insurance Threatens to Break Down 1

Chapter 2
Insolvency-Resolution Policies of the Deposit Insurance Agencies 31

Chapter 3
Structural Weaknesses in the U.S. Deposit Insurance System 59

Chapter 4
Current Exposure of Deposit Insurance Agencies to Interest Volatility Risk 87

Chapter 5
Emerging Risks and the Deposit Insurance Subsidy 119

Chapter 6
Proposals to Reduce FDIC and FSLIC Subsidies to Deposit Institution Risk-Taking 145

Index 167

Series Foreword

Government regulation of economic activity in the United States has grown dramatically in this century, radically transforming government-business relations. Economic regulation of prices and conditions of service was first applied to transportation and public utilities and was later extended to energy, health care, and other sectors. In the early 1970s explosive growth occurred in social regulation, focusing on workplace safety, environmental preservation, consumer protection, and related goals. Though regulatory reform has occupied a prominent place on the agendas of recent administrations, and some important reforms have occurred, the aims, methods, and results of many regulatory programs remain controversial.

The purpose of the MIT Press series, Regulation of Economic Activity, is to inform the ongoing debate on regulatory policy by making significant and relevant research available to both scholars and decision makers. Books in this series present new insights into individual agencies, programs, and regulated sectors, as well as the important economic, political, and administrative aspects of the regulatory process that cut across these boundaries.

The provision of financial services has been pervasively regulated in the United States since the 1930s. Until quite recently this regulation has not received scholarly attention commensurate with its economic importance; it seemed to fall into a large crack, separating students of regulation, whose backgrounds rarely equipped them to analyze financial markets, and students of finance, who were not generally much interested in regulation and its effects. Happily, this unnatural gap has narrowed in recent years, and this study should help to narrow it further.

Many observers have argued for removal of much of the regulation of financial services that was imposed in the 1930s. But few have advocated abolition of the important legacy of the New Deal that Edward Kane studies here: federal deposit insurance programs. These programs are traditionally praised for having increased public confidence in banks and in savings and loan associations (a very important objective in the

Depression) and for having prevented runs on these institutions. But Kane points out that these programs also have had costs that have not been fully appreciated. Particularly, as currently operated, federal insurance schemes give deposit institutions excessive incentives to acquire risky assets. This point and its implications under current market conditions are developed fully, and a set of thoughtful reform proposals are made. This study should be of interest to scholars and decision makers concerned with financial markets and their regulation, as well as to students of regulation who have not yet discovered this important research area.

Richard Schmalensee

Acknowledgments

For convincing me to write this book, I thank Lawrence S. Ritter and James M. Kemper, Jr.

For penetrating criticism of an early draft of this manuscript, I am deeply grateful to Richard Aspinwall, Robert Eisenbeis, Alan Marcus, J. Huston McCulloch, Joseph F. Sinkey, Jr., Robert Taggart, and an anonymous reader for The MIT Press. On specific chapters of this same manuscript, I received valuable suggestions from Curt Hunter, Ronald Masulis, James Moser, and Leonard Simon. I also acknowledge the role played in the evolution of my thinking by conversations with all of these gentlemen and also with George Benston, Gerald Bierwag, Andrew Chen, Jack Guttentag, Benson Hart, Patric Hendershott, George Kaufman, David Pyle, Myron Scholes, Robert Van Order, and Kevin Villani.

For research assistance, I am indebted to James Moser, who compiled the first versions of many of the tables presented in chapters 3 and 4. For information about SEC regulation of bank holding companies, I am grateful to Charles Cox and Annette Poulsen of the Securities and Exchange Commission. I also thank Stanley Silverberg and Patrick Golodner of the Federal Deposit Insurance Corporation, William Gavin of the Federal Reserve Bank of Cleveland, and Henry Cassidy, Dorothy DeLong, Richard Pickering, Virginia Olin, and Steve Zabrenski of the Federal Home Loan Bank Board for helping me to obtain unpublished data. Appreciation is also due to Patricia Akison for the skill and good humor with which she word processed innumerable drafts of this study.

Finally, my warmest thanks go to my wife Gloria and our children Laura, Stephen, and Ted for permitting me to devote so many evenings and weekends to this manuscript.

The Gathering Crisis in Federal Deposit Insurance

Chapter 1

Why Federal Deposit Insurance Threatens to Break Down

This book seeks to change the way the reader thinks about federal deposit insurance. It looks at deposit insurance not from the point of view of a prospective beneficiary but from the point of view of a taxpayer who—through higher taxes, inflation, or user fees—will be called upon to make good the financially staggering amount of the system's guarantees. Far from celebrating the past crises that deposit insurance has spared us, the book emphasizes the past regulatory decisions about how to handle actual and potential insolvencies at individual deposit institutions have taken a largely unrecognized toll on both the aggregate value of implicit federal obligations and the riskiness of contemporary financial institutions.

The book's theme is that the system of federal deposit insurance adopted during the 1930s is becoming as dangerous and as unreliable as an old and undermaintained automobile. This metaphor is instructive if only because the behavior of such cars is a subject about which most of us gain considerable expertise. While the deposit insurance automobile is still adequate for light loads in flat country, it cannot be driven endlessly up and down steep interest-rate mountains without breaking down. There is good reason to doubt either that the old car has many more interest-rate mountains left in it or that it can be steered unharmed through the mine field of contemporary financial services competition. Subsequent chapters develop evidence to support the aptness of this metaphor. To let us examine this evidence unemotionally, it is useful to clear away some potentially disturbing questions:

1. How could elected officials let these problems develop? Why don't they fix or replace the system before a breakdown occurs?
2. What would the breakdown look like? Who would get hurt?
3. Why do failures of insured deposit institutions drag deposit insurers into trouble?
4. What types of changes would improve the system?

1. *How could elected officials let the value of deposit insurance guarantees lurch out of control? Why don't they fix or replace the system before a breakdown occurs?*

The answer to the first set of questions lies in the human mind's penchant for responding to fearful prospects by simple denial. Most of us instinctively refuse to face unpleasant evidence squarely. Anyone who has ever broken a bone or suffered a deep cut knows that our first impulse is to deny that *we* could ever suffer so serious an injury. The breakdown of deposit insurance is so disruptive an event that everyone desperately wants to believe that it cannot happen. As the little boy said to Shoeless Joe Jackson at the onset of the Black Sox Scandal, "Say it ain't so, Joe."

Elected politicians have extra incentives to deny that serious problems exist. First, facing up to the problem would force them to accept some of the blame for allowing the situation to deteriorate so badly. Second, to make things right, they would have to take actions that would redistribute wealth away from some of their supporting constituencies. Either action could adversely affect their chances of winning reelection.

Policymakers' denial of the deposit insurance problem means that instead of using the time provided by the largely downhill interest-rate ride of 1982–1983 to make needed repairs, the administration and Congress spent the time congratulating themselves and their drivers for keeping the deposit insurance car from being shaken apart by two patches of particularly rough road traversed in the last five years: the problems of thrift institution insolvency and de facto defaults on commercial bank loans to less-developed countries and to agricultural and energy firms in this country. Since 1981 these problems have kept many large and small deposit institutions under continual pressure.

Chapter 4 develops data that indicate that the net worth accounts of thrift institutions have sunk deeply underwater in market value. Even when interest rates declined in 1983, many deposit institutions remained underwater. At best they floated near enough to the surface to emit visible bubbles. On average during 1982–1984, one savings and loan association (S&L) and one commercial bank have failed every week. In the second half of 1984 the failure rate was running even higher. In 1983 the list of problem banks maintained by the Federal Deposit Insurance Corporation (FDIC) grew by 25 institutions per month. Despite reaching record levels, in 1984 it was still increasing by about three banks a week. The size of receivership assets owned by the FDIC is approaching $10 billion, and the caseload of creditor lawsuits against which the FDIC must defend itself is growing by thousands of cases per year. Even though the Federal Savings and Loan Insurance Corporation (FSLIC) does not maintain a parallel list of problem S&Ls, the hangover of low-interest-rate mortgages on the books of S&Ls and mutual savings banks (MSBs) means that rising interest rates in the first half of 1984 drove the market value of the assets of the firms it insures many billions of dollars farther underwater.

In the face of these developments, it is hard to understand why many economists continue to praise the federal deposit insurance system as the single unqualifiedly successful financial policy innovation to come out of the 1930s. The issue is whether the system's obvious successes in the flat country of 1933–1965 are sustainable in the mountainous land of contemporary times.

In 1933 the institution of federal deposit insurance helped to restore public confidence in the U.S. system of deposit institutions. But over time agency personnel performed this task too zealously. Misguided but understandable efforts to paper over the current costs of failure resolution lulled many uninsured creditors of deposit institutions into the mistaken presumption that, except for scattered closings of small firms, deposit institution failures were a thing of the past. For the first four decades after 1933 the nation's avoidance of failures among large institutions—and indeed of widespread deposit runs or failures of any kind—fostered the illusion that federal deposit insurance is a miraculously low-cost device for ensuring a stable system of financial intermediation.

We may exploit our automotive metaphor to demonstrate the danger inherent in this illusion by recalling a famous series of television commercials for Fram oil filters. In these commercials a mechanic who holds a broken piston in one hand and a Fram oil filter in the other observes that drivers can either pay him now or pay him later. Like a procrastinating motorist, FDIC and FSLIC cost accounting makes a myopic trade-off between paying for routine maintenance now and paying for heavy repairs later. The true costs of resolving past deposit insurance problems are much greater than the accounting record reveals. The more experience deposit institutions have had with the system, the more leverage, default, and interest-rate risk they have sought to load into the deposit insurance jalopy. This makes for good downhill riding but strains the brakes on curves and overloads the motor on grades.

The point that authorities don't want to face is that, however well the deposit insurance system may have run in the past, it is headed for a bureaucratic breakdown. It's not a case of "If it ain't broke, don't fix it." Unless market discipline is reimposed on deposit institution risk-taking, the deposit insurance bureaucracy will seize up at a most inopportune time.

2. What would happen if Federal deposit insurance reserves were suddenly exhausted?

It is unlikely that insured customers would suffer long-lasting losses or inconvenience in a deposit insurance breakdown. Although such problems are not totally out of the question, the politics of central banking and deposit institution regulation make it unlikely. Congress has already passed a joint resolution putting the "full faith and credit" of the federal government behind insurance agency guarantees. But because the resolution fails to indicate how the government's blanket obligation is to be discharged, a sudden nationwide run on troubled deposit institutions (a widespread, panicky effort by deposit institution customers to withdraw their funds from many of the weakest institutions in the system) could temporarily exhaust deposit insurance reserves and cause some wild bureaucratic scrambling if Congress feels the need at that moment to debate how best to make good its guarantees.

To appreciate how politically disruptive a shortage of deposit insurance reserves can be, we may look at the reactions of politicians, depositors, and state-insured institutions in Nebraska to the November 1983 insolvency of the Nebraska Depository Institutions Guaranty Corporation. This case represents a microcosm of the pressures that would develop if federal deposit insurance broke down. The insolvency occurred when the claims generated by the November 1, 1983, failure of $67 million

Commonwealth Savings Company, a state-chartered industrial bank ineligible for FDIC insurance, came up against a $2 million state insurance fund. Estimates of the liquidation value of Commonwealth assets leave the bank's 6,700 depositors holding the bag for between $25 million and $47 million in uncollectible deposits and suffering a serious loss of liquidity in having to wait out the liquidation process. Aggrieved depositors brought suit against the state of Nebraska on the grounds that the state had failed to stop its banking department and insurance agency from following "willful, wanton, or fraudulent" policies. In June 1984 a state claims board held the state liable for $33 million. Among its other findings, the board judged the state to be negligent in allowing Commonwealth to join the guaranty corporation in 1979 and in raising the fund's account-level guarantees from $10,000 to $30,000 per account in 1980. Before depositors can collect from the state, however, this finding must be approved by a district court and the necessary funds must be appropriated by the legislature. As one would expect, legislative debate over how to raise the funds to finance such an appropriation pits various groups of potential taxpayers against each other and threatens to end the political careers of important incumbent politicians. Realistically the issue is how to divide the cost of the bailout between special taxes levied on surviving financial institutions in the state and various forms of general taxation. Surviving financial institutions were affected by the failure in other ways too. In the immediate wake of the insolvency, other state-insured industrial banks had to scramble to arrange alternative forms of cover. They found this cover either in the FSLIC, in a strong acquirer, or in the protections offered by a bankruptcy court.

At the federal level the ability to create money makes subsidized emergency loans to threatened institutions a quick and politically easy way to arrest any systemic run on deposit institutions. But repeated doses of bailout medicines run the risk of cumulating into a de facto nationalization of the deposit institution industry. This is the bottom line to the incipient crisis, one whose difficulties and inevitability are foreshadowed in two other recent cases.

The first case is that of so-called S&L phoenix institutions: seven large FSLIC-owned (i.e., implicitly nationalized) S&Ls created in the early 1980s by supervisory mergers of two or more failing S&Ls that happened to be located in the same geographical area. Like the mythical phoenix itself, these institutions sprang from the ashes of their predecessor firms' previous existence. Government operation was adopted as a way of resolving the imminent failure of the component associations in the absence of attractive takeover bids from private parties. To avoid a write-down of its insurance reserves, the FSLIC put funds and new management into the phoenixes and waited for a more favorable opportunity to sell its equity stake. At year-end 1982, one phoenix had been sold, and the remaining phoenixes aggregated about $18 billion in assets (Guttentag 1984). In August 1984 three phoenixes had still not been sold back to the private sector: Talman Home Federal (Chicago), First Federal of Rochester, and First Federal Savings Bank of Puerto Rico. At year-end 1983 these institutions had $11.5 billion in assets. Delays in liquidating FSLIC equity positions, phoenix managers' allegations of excessive regulatory interference, and complaints from competing enterprises that phoenix institutions enjoyed unfair exemptions from antitrust restrictions underscore the temptations and difficulties that even a temporary nationalization imposes.

The second case is the FDIC's July 1984 takeover of 80 percent of the stock in the Continental Illinois Bank and Trust Company. As in the phoenix nationalizations, private parties failed to make an attractive bid for the failing firm, and administrators of deposit insurance reserves saw nationalization as preferable to liquidating the firm's assets and liabilities. Nationalization appeared bureaucratically less embarrassing than accepting an appropriately large write-down of the insurer's accumulated reserve funds.

Selling off the FDIC's and FSLIC's stake in a few institutions has proved to be a slow and painful business. Selling off at a politically nonembarrassing price and without corruption a parallel stake in the hundreds of institutions that might be acquired in the course of a full-fledged deposit insurance crisis might not even prove a manageable undertaking. Even if a full-fledged deposit insurance crisis can be avoided, the equity stake inherent in the value of deposit insurance guarantees is growing rapidly. History tells us that whatever activities a government supports, it eventually strives to control.

3. Why do deposit institution failures drag deposit insurers into trouble? Deposit institution failure is a morbid topic. Like the death of a valued citizen, the failure of a deposit institution has unpleasant consequences for a number of parties: stockholders, employees, suppliers, customers, and—because deposit institution soundness is a major regulatory responsibility—deposit institution regulators.

Deposit institutions fail because they are in the business of taking risks. No matter how well they choose these risks, events cannot always turn out favorably. Still, whenever a series of failures occurs or strongly threatens, deposit institution regulators are made to share the blame with deposit institution managers. Regulators are criticized for lacking vigilance: for failing to curb at least the boldest forms of failed institutions' unsuccessful risk-taking. At such times the intensity of public criticism rises with the number and aggregate size of the institutions perceived to be in danger of failure.

Regulators' economic responsibilities and political interest in minimizing public criticism lead them to adopt policies for preventing, detecting, and resolving individual insolvencies and for arresting their spread to additional institutions. Risk-control programs aimed at individual institutions include restrictions on portfolio composition and record keeping, surprise examination of the condition of individual institutions, careful management of the information assembled in these examinations, and pressure on managers to correct abusive and unsound practices and to strengthen institutional balance sheets. In pursuing these policies, regulators labor at an informational disadvantage. They operate on the opposite side of a regulatory game board from deposit institution managers who reap benefits from concealing their firm's problems from the regulators' view. Hiding problems postpones the imposition of regulatory penalties, buying time for daring new business strategies to succeed and for asset values to be restored by favorable movements in interest rates.

Risks that Individual Deposit Instutions Take

Risk attaches to any project that exposes the value of one's human or nonhuman wealth to a chance of future losses. The word *chance* makes it clear that the outcome of a risky project or opportunity cannot be fully predictable. Owning a deposit institution exposes a stockholder to unpredictable variability in the market value of the institution (Rosenberg and Perry 1978). This market value may be conceived as capital: the difference between the aggregate value of the financial and physical assets owned by the institution and the aggregate value of its nonequity liabilities. For a deposit institution's stockholders and uninsured creditors, portfolio risk comes from two separate sources: from fluctuations in the values of the financial assets and liabilities that a firm books as an institutional investor and from fluctuations in the value of the physical assets it holds as a producer and deliverer of financial services. We call the first class of portfolio risk a firm's *financial risk* and apply the term *service facility risk* to the second type.

Both classes of risk may be sliced into separable layers of risk exposure that we may associate with management decisions about the level of risk accepted in different aspects of a deposit institution's business activities (Sinkey 1985). As depicted in figure 1.1, financial risk may be sorted into six categories: internal integrity risk, affiliated institution risk, liquidity risk, credit risk, interest rate risk, and foreign exchange risk. Service facility risk may be separated into operating efficiency risk, regulatory risk, and technology risk.

Some sources of risk are managed differently from others. In particular managers are expected to adopt policies to minimize uncertainty about the internal integrity and operating efficiency of the organization they head; however, the object is to control rather than to avoid other forms of risk. For bearing voluntary forms of risk, managers are expected to position the firm so that it promises to reap a creditable return. Tools for managing risk include: reserve positioning; lines of credit; credit investigation; portfolio, locational, and technological diversification; techniques for correcting mismatches in the maturity profiles of assets and liabilities; and research and planning directed at predicting and coping with technological and regulatory change.

Why Federal Deposit Insurance Threatens to Break Down 9

Financial risk

Risk of breakdowns in the firm's system for encouraging internal integrity	Risk of losses passed along from affiliated (including subsidiary) institutions	Liquidity risk: the risk that servicing an unpredictable surge in net clearings and cash withdrawals will impose substantial expenses on the firm	Credit risk: the risk that borrowers will default on promised repayments	Interest volatility risk: the risk that changes in the level of market interest rate will affect the market value of assets and liabilities differently	Foreign exchange risk: the risk of unfavorable fluctuations in the value of assets and liabilities denominated in foreign currencies

Service facility risk

Risk that the firm will operate at less than maximum efficiency	Risk that unforeseen regulatory action will impair the firm's profitability	Risks that changes in technological opportunities will reduce the value of the firm's existing systems for producing and delivering financial services

Figure 1.1 Components of portfolio risk for a deposit institution

Resulting Systemic Risks of Individual Failures Triggering a Chain Reaction

Insuring depositors of a single institution against loss is conceptually more straightforward than insuring a system of institutions. Sinkey (1979, p. 5) observes the "misuse of banking resources by inept or dishonest managers has been the major cause of bank failures (except, of course, during periods of severe economic depression)."

When a federal agency undertakes to insure a network of deposit institutions, it must worry also about the statistical independence of financial risks and service facility risks across the universe of individual firms it insures. Agency management must both assess and (so far as it can) control the risk that individual failures might accumulate into a systemic event. Elected politicians reveal themselves to be less interested in how efficiently the FDIC and FSLIC handle the failures of individual institutions in the long run than in whether they maintain public confidence in deposit institutions during their current term in office. At the FDIC and FSLIC the overriding goal is to keep difficulties experienced by individual institutions from spreading in epidemic fashion to other members of the depository institution system.

Because deposit insurance in an individual institution protects depositors up to $100,000 per account name, the vast majority of U.S. citizens need worry about deposit institution failures only when economic information makes the threat of widespread insolvency seem very real. This insight leads deposit institution lobbyists to view the task of arresting the development and spread of deposit institution failures as a matter of minimizing not merely managerial mistakes but even bad publicity. Until the 1970s specialized state and federal regulatory authorities for deposit institutions determinedly sheltered poorly managed institutions from unfavorable publicity. They feared that bad news about a deposit institution might increase its chance of failure by driving away uninsured depositors and other creditors.

Even today regulator-approved accounting principles make economic and legal insolvency conceptually distinct events. De facto or market-value insolvency exists when an institution no longer has the resources to meet its contractual obligations. This occurs when the market value of its assets falls below the market value of its liabilities. Legal insolvency occurs when an institution cannot cover its current liabilities. In contrast to both of these conditions, failure occurs when the insolvency is officially recognized by the institution's chartering agency and the firm is closed by supervisory action or involuntarily merged out of existence. Especially for large firms, regulators ordinarily make a tenacious effort through subsidized lending to keep troubled institutions afloat well past the point of market value insolvency. In cases where de jure insolvency either is or becomes inevitable, they endeavor as a matter of policy to effect the closing in a way that, compared to liquidating the assets of the failing firm, minimizes the chance of undermining public confidence in other deposit institutions.

Because performance of insurance agency bureaucrats is not judged by agency profits, minimizing an already small probability of contagion typically seems preferable to minimizing the solely economic costs of individual failures. Immediate damage to other parties is lessened in two ways: by delaying the closing until holders of uninsured debt have had time either to liquidate or to insulate their claims and by being prepared to assist a stronger institution to absorb the failing firm and assume full responsibility for its outstanding debt contracts. This policy effectively invests some of the immediately salvageable value of the insurance agency's claim on the resources of the failing firm in supervisory activity aimed at minimizing the number of failures actually observed. In staking the continued play of failing institutions with insurance agency money, regulators force the taxpayer to hold the downside of their portfolio bets. The interests of the taxpayer would be better served by a profit-maximizing insurer who would take over the upside, too.

For an insurance company, notice periods for cancelling insurance coverage (and, for a lender, contractual rights for foreclosing on the assets of an insolvent client) constitute important means for limiting its exposure to risk-taking that is initiated voluntarily by its clients. Information management is also conceived as an important element in federal risk management and failure prevention policies. Accurate and timely information on deposit institution risk-taking would allow customers and investors to penalize overly risky behavior. However, even for well-run deposit institutions, truly adequate information on the quality of assets and operating policies is hard to come by. Almost without exception and with regulatory connivance, financial statements published for deposit institutions are exercises in cosmetic accounting.

When deposit institutions are closely held, cosmetic accounting may serve stockholder interests. But as deposit institution ownership has broadened and particularly as it has become layered through holding companies (corporations formed to own the stock of other corporations), minority owners have often been placed at a scandalous disadvantage. As the U.S. banking system switched increasingly to holding company ownership in the late 1960s, Securities and Exchange Commission (SEC) jurisdiction over securities issued by large, publicly held bank holding companies (those with over 300 shareholders and over $3 million in assets) permitted it to require disclosure of adverse information by major banks. (In addition, holding companies with at least 500 shareholders and those that are registered on a national exchange are subject to SEC restrictions on corporate governance.) The SEC has required large bank holding companies to disclose nonperforming loans since 1976, asset liability mismatching since 1980, and problems with foreign loans since October 1982. Market participants' judicious response to this information and the Reagan administration's announced preference for deregulation have led agencies directly responsible for deposit institution regulation and the interagency Federal Financial Institutions Examination Council to consider numerous proposals for additional disclosure. Nevertheless, examiner reports and ratings are not ordinarily available for public scrutiny. Damage control recordkeeping, which focuses on book rather than market values of assets and liabilities, makes unfavorable information all the more dramatic when it does surface. With uninsured creditors and minority stockholders having much at stake and little reliable information, adverse rumors about a deposit institution's condition sometimes trigger substantial outflows of deposit and nondeposit funds and declines in the market value of the firm's stock. For example, in four months in 1984 Continental Illinois lost more than 25 percent of its private funding and roughly 80 percent of its stock value.

When such problems become epidemic as in 1933, restoring public confidence in deposit institutions becomes an urgent political problem. At such times fundamental changes in regulatory arrangements are adopted, often with greater concern for their dramatic immediate effect than for their long-run consequences. Regulatory reforms that are so conceived take their place among the causes both of an immediate economic recovery and in time of the next banking crisis.

Some Unpleasant Effects of Deposit Insurance

Far from eliminating the risk of deposit institution insolvency, deposit insurance merely shifts the burden of portfolio risk from deposit institutions and their creditors to other parties in society. Moreover, unless it is properly priced, deposit insurance actually increases aggregate deposit institution risk-taking. Which sectors ultimately bear the burden of deposit institution risk depends on the system of deposit insurance pricing and the methods that deposit insurance agencies use to resolve de facto client insolvencies when they occur. Analysis indicates that, under current arrangements, the burden of backing up insurance agency deposit guarantees falls principally on the insurance system's implicit guarantors: the general taxpayer and conservatively managed institutions able to survive whatever crisis might unfold.

Today the aggregate value of deposit insurance guarantees is much larger than is generally recognized and is administratively out of control. This lack of control and the distribution of the implicit responsibility for backstopping the system's unfunded guarantees is neither economically nor politically sustainable. The danger is that by the time the issue is openly confronted, U.S. deposit institutions may find that—without anyone's ever intending it—exercising the system's option to take over an insolvent deposit institution industry may have become the only politically expedient way to settle accounts.

This back-door path to nationalizing deposit institutions is being paved by systematically mispricing deposit insurance services. In what is a world of rapid change, current arrangements offer clients essentially free coverage for unfamiliar types of risk-taking. Newly emerging varieties of deposit institution risk—such as those generated by asset and liability product line expansion and extensions in geographic market area accomplished through holding company affiliates—are neither explicitly nor implicitly priced by deposit insurance authorities. Unpriced risks tempt managers of insured institutions to occupy a more hazardous portfolio position that their unsubsidized tolerance for risk would otherwise support.

Arbitrage possibilities exist whenever a good or service has a different price or anticipated rate of return in two markets. If transactions costs were zero, one could earn a riskless profit by buying (going long) in the high return market and covering this position by selling (going short) in the low return one. However, an insured institution cannot arbitrage the price of risk-bearing services between asset and deposit insurance markets without exposing itself to a definite risk of failure. This is because deposit insurance agencies are not legally required to make payments unless and until a client's own resources are exhausted. To arbitrage the price of deposit insurance, a deposit institution manager must go long in opportunities whose riskiness is less than fully priced by his or her insurance agency and dare to cover this risk by giving the insurer the right to take over his firm when and if its net worth becomes inadequate. Such arbitrage shifts the burden for underwriting an insured institution's catastrophic losses onto the agency's insurance reserves.

Deposit insurance arbitrage illustrates every insurance fund's exposure to moral hazard. Dictionaries define *moral hazard* as an insurance company's risk as to the insured's trustworthiness and honesty. This definition construes moral hazard literally, as the chance of unethical behavior by an insured. But except for explaining the etymological origin of the term, this definition is outdated. In contemporary usage the meaning of *moral* is stretched to cover any self-interested voluntary response to an insurance contract by an insured (Mayers and Smith 1982). Moral hazard exists because of differences in the risk-taking incentives that would confront an insured and an uninsured party that are identical except in their insurance coverage. Conflicts between the interests of the two parties to an insurance contract mean that, like acrobats working with the benefit of a safety net, insureds can afford to be more daring than they could if they were not able to rely on insurance coverage to truncate their losses. An insurance company's moral hazard resides in the power that its clients retain to pursue risks that willfully increase the value of their side of an insurance deal, thereby lowering net expected benefits to the insurance company.

Because the early success of the federal deposit insurance system increased customer and managerial confidence in that system, it encouraged managers to adopt progressively bolder attitudes toward portfolio risk. In the 1970s and early 1980s examples of this phenomenon can be found in aggressive commercial bank lending both to independent operators in the energy field and to governments and governmental enterprises in less-developed and Eastern European countries.

Preventing Deposit Insurance Failures: Examination, Disclosure, and Strengthening Policies

In line with the maxim that an ounce of prevention is worth a pound of cure, deposit insurance agencies emphasize client surveillance. The bulk of their labor force consists of examiners who, making little use of modern information and telecommunications technology, review data from call reports and periodically visit client institutions to evaluate the quality of their loan portfolios and management practices. Although responsibility for preserving depositors' wealth rests with the deposit insurance agencies, authority to conduct on-site examinations is shared bureaucratically with chartering authorities (state banking commissions and the U.S. Comptroller of the Currency) and the Federal Reserve System. Principles and standards for federal examinations are being standardized by the five-agency Federal Financial Institutions Examination Council. This Council was established by the Financial Institution and Interest Rate Control Act of 1978 to coordinate the regulatory activities of five federal deposit institution regulators: the Fed, the Comptroller, the FDIC, the Federal Home Loan Bank Board (FHLBB), and the National Credit Union Administration. But progress toward coordination has been slow due to differences in the distribution of the costs and benefits of regulatory change across individual agencies and to continued skirmishing over bureaucratic turf.

Reports from on-site examinations focus on the adequacy or inadequacy of the firm's capital account for meeting the particular forms of risk exposure that worry examiners. Traditionally examiners have devoted their attention primarily to risks from nonperforming and questionable loans (Spong and Hoenig 1979) and secondarily to risks from problems rooted in management competence and integrity. Examination reports feature recommendations for changes in management practices designed to improve the institution's performance and for increases in capital meant to strengthen the institution's balance sheet.

Strategically examiners have the task of uncovering problem institutions before their situation declines to the point where future losses threaten to exceed the privately supplied equity of the firm and tap into the resources of the deposit insurance agencies. Although in special cases a problem classification may trace to corruption or gross risk-taking of another sort, examiners typically conceive a problem institution as one whose capital is low relative to potential default losses on outstanding loans (Sinkey 1979). Because it ignores several important sources of risk displayed in figure 1.1, this conception of deposit institution risk is dangerously outmoded. Like the institution of federal deposit insurance itself, examination procedures are rooted in a 1930s conception of what causes bank failures. They implicitly embody the view that because loans are the chief asset of deposit institutions, and except for losses due to theft and embezzlement, institutions find themselves in irremediable trouble only when borrowers prove unable to service outstanding loan agreements. Besides risks from crime and customer defaults, examiners today must confront the possibility of losses caused by interest volatility, movements in foreign exchange rates, political developments in foreign countries, and technological obsolescence. To be maximally effective, examiners must adaptively identify and evaluate new forms of risk as they emerge.

To protect client institutions from unfavorable publicity, cosmetic accounting is permitted and examination reports and agencies' lists of problem institutions held from public view. This pursuit of administrative secrecy contrasts sharply with the openness emphasized by the SEC. The keystone of the SEC's approach to regulating securities activity is government-mandated disclosure of potentially relevant financial information that can allow outside investors to form accurate assessments of the value of specific securities. Deposit institutions and their specialized federal regulators have argued continually among themselves and with the SEC over proposals to require increased disclosure of information on problem loans and balance sheet structure.

In the 1980s, as financial services institutions became more and more alike and public support for deposit institution deregulation developed, proposals for disclosing problem conditions gained considerable momentum. Bank holding companies and deposit institutions that engage in brokerage activities fall under the disclosure regulations of the SEC. The SEC requires a growing number of specified bank holding companies (between April 1983 and July 1984, the number grew from 553 to 981) to discuss mismatches between the maturities of their assets and liabilities in their annual reports. In October 1982 it mandated that bank holding companies disclose information on significant loans and investments (those constituting more than 1 percent of outstanding assets) in countries experiencing so-called liquidity problems. Even more recently it announced plans to require figures for foreign and domestic nonperforming loans to be divulged separately.

Specialized deposit institution regulators have begun to follow the SEC's lead. In December 1982 the Comptroller of the Currency and the head of the FDIC separately espoused the principle that releasing more information about the operations of individual banks would help to check excessive risk-taking by increasing the effectiveness of market discipline on risky banks. In particular they have stepped up enforcement actions against banks that fail to report accurate financial information to depositors and stockholders. In mid-1983 federal regulators began to publish information on loans that are ninety or more days past due, on nonaccruing loans, and on troubled debt restructurings. They are also encouraging insured banks and thrifts to make additional disclosures voluntarily and considering requiring public audits of bank financial statements, announcing disciplinary actions taken against individual banks, and disclosing the weaknesses regulatory personnel uncover in the course of periodic examinations.

Deposit Insurers: Fly Now, Pay Later

Over time the true cost of financing federal deposit insurance has incrased massively and become increasingly inequitable in its distribution.

Correspondingly the formal protection against deposit institution failures that the system is supposed to provide has begun to wear thin. Beginning in the mid-1970s a wave of failures among large institutions started the nation on a course of reality therapy. By 1980 deposit institution balance sheets reeked of de facto insolvency. They contained unrealized losses whose realization would swamp not only the industry's accumulated net worth but even the reserves of federal deposit insurance agencies. For the first time since the 1930s the rate of failure of U.S. deposit institutions surfaced as a regular subject for cocktail-party inquiry.

Perhaps surprisingly the basic difficulties were clearly foreseen in the debate that preceded the establishment of the federal deposit insurance system. Deposit insurance occupied a place on the national agenda for roughly a century before its adoption in 1933. State experiments with insuring bank obligations (bank notes as well as deposits) extend back to 1829. In Congress the legislative history includes the introduction of 150 bills providing for federal guarantees or insurance of bank deposits, dating as far back as 1886. These bills are analyzed in detail in the FDIC's *Annual Report* for 1950 (pp. 63–101), and the FDIC's *Annual Report* for 1952 (pp. 59–71) summarizes the structure and operating experience of the fourteen state insurance systems established betwen 1829 and 1917.

Legislators resisted federal deposit insurance so long because insight derived from the experience of defunct state deposit insurance funds and from economic analysis showed it to be menaced by twin problems of economic inefficiency and uneven incidence in benefits and costs. Economists noted that unless insurance assessments were related to the risks taken by individual banks, deposit guarantees eventually would foster looser banking practices rather than sounder ones. In one of the first published analyses of the federal deposit insurance system, Emerson (1934) made this point with disconcerting force. Economists also expressed the fear that the benefits and costs of federal guarantees would be unfairly distributed. Early observers predicted that deposit insurance would subsidize small and weak banks at the expense of large and strong ones (Emerson 1934; Golembe 1960; Burns 1974; Green 1981). Many saw this distributional effect as inefficiently retarding the development of systems of wide-area branch banking in regions where branch office networks would be socially beneficial.

While events have confirmed the dangers of setting insurance premiums that are not risk-rated, the precise scenario that unfolded differed in three ways from the one envisioned by the system's early critics. First, although from the beginning managers of deposit insurance agencies have proved unwilling to undertake the difficult administrative task of setting risk-rated explicit premiums, they discovered that their resources would soon be swamped if they did not erect regulatory incentives to limit client venturesomeness. Effectively the agencies use state and federal examiners to enforce a risk-rated structure of implicit premiums. They accomplish this by imposing escalating administrative penalties on institutions whose operating policies or portfolio positions are recognized as risky by examiners. The rub in this approach is that the mix of political and economic incentives that governs the behavior of government bureaucrats greatly lengthens the inevitable lag of examiner recognition behind the true importance of emerging forms of yet-to-be-regulated risk. In recent years this delay is exemplified by regulators' slowness to regulate interest volatility risk, liquidity risk from standby commitments, credit risk from loans to sovereign governments and government-owned corporations in other countries (against which traditional lender remedies such as judgments and foreclosure rights are hard to enforce), and service facility risk associated with technological change. Regulatory lags amplify incentives for clients to invent and to pursue new and unregulated forms of portfolio risks. If their agency's economic viability were not backstopped by other federal resources, deposit insurers would have to take cognizance much sooner of emerging risks.

Second, as predicted, conservatively managed deposit institutions find themselves paying too much for deposit insurance, while institutions that aggressively pursue unregulated risks pay too little. But in an adaptive world inequities in the distribution of the burden of financing the deposit insurance system could not permanently turn on the size of client portfolios. The unwillingness of the FDIC to permit uninsured creditors to suffer the consequences of a large-bank failure and evidence on the pattern of short-funding and intercountry lending observed for banks in different size classes indicate that banks in the nation's largest size class faced strong incentives to develop a subsidized exposure to unregulated risks.

Third, by designing strategically located networks of subsidiaries that possess complementary banking powers, bank holding companies have been able to establish, with little loss of economic efficiency, a banking presence across state boundaries.

Failure, Insolvency, and Deposit Institution Net Worth

In choosing to fly now and pay later, deposit insurers have nurtured an essentially artificial distinction between the insolvency and the failure of an insured institution. Failure is marked by a suspension of autonomous operations, an event that requires discretionary action by an institution's chartering authority. Insolvency occurs whenever an institution's nonownership liabilities exceed its assets. A finding of at least potential insolvency is a necessary condition for declaring a failure, but even in the face of a strong evidence of market value insolvency, failure is an administrative option that a supervisory authority may or may not choose to exercise.

Regulators seldom declare a deposit institution insolvent just because it reaches a condition where the *market value* of its net worth ceases to be positive. In 1938 the three federal banking agencies and supervisors of state banks agreed to value reasonably risky marketable securities at cost and to carry loans at par as long as ultimate repayment was "reasonably assured" (Klebaner 1974, p. 161). Hence the only category of an institution's unrealized losses that currently enter regulatory appraisals of deposit institution solvency is losses projected on assets that are classified unfavorably by deposit institution examiners. De jure insolvency occurs only when the chartering authority certifies formally that the book value of an institution's capital resources has been exhausted by a combination of operating losses, assets disallowed by examiners worried about default risk, and losses recognized either from asset sales or from employee theft.

A problem institution fails when it is closed or involuntarily merged out of existence. Closing requires the state commission or federal agency that chartered a firm to decide (often under the urging of the deposit insurance agency involved) that its normal attitude of administrative forbearance is no longer in its bureaucratic interest. The deposit insurance agency's strongest independent sanction is merely to threaten to institute proceedings to terminate the institution's insured status. Typically an institution's insurance agency and chartering authority review a problem situation for a long while before deciding to merge or to close a troubled firm. As an alternative to failure, the insurer may offer financial assistance or request that the institution raise additional capital or make specified changes in management or management policies.

An individual deposit institution's risk of failure is rooted in its management and in its balance sheet. Particularly relevant are the exposure of its loans to default, mismatches between the time profiles of its assets and liabilities, and the extent to which it has leveraged its accumulated capital resources. Risks of deposit institution failure rose during the 1970s and early 1980s for two reasons.

First, many deposit institution managers voluntarily embraced unregulated forms of portfolio risk as a way to increase the anticipated return on equity capital paid by their firm. To increase their prospective lending margins, deposit institution managers made riskier loans and financed these loans in riskier fashion. They spread their earnings over a smaller equity base and funded their holdings of assets with liabilities that promised to roll over on average well before (or in some cases well after) the assets matured.

Second, the risk of existing deposit institution portfolios shot upward with the sudden increase in the volatility of interest rates shown in figures 1.2 and 1.3. Interest rate swings shown in figure 1.2 are much wider after October 6, 1979, than before. Figure 1.3 reports moving average values for mean squared variation in bill and bond rates over twelve-month periods. Both graphs confirm that a break occurred in the structure of these interest rate series in late 1979.

This break in economic structure was brought about by the October 6, 1979, change in operative monetary policy strategies. The increase in interest volatility and the long recession that began soon after caused an across-the-board rise in the riskiness of preexisting asset-liability

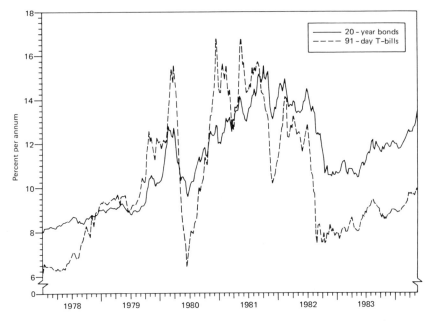

Figure 1.2 October 1979 shift in volatility of interest rates on U.S. Treasury bills and bonds

mismatches, in the value of depositor options to draw down passbook and checking account funds, and in customer default rates on loans. These developments underscore the nonrandom role of macroeconomic policy decisions in interest volatility risk. Deposit institutions' exposure to discretionary macroeconomic policy risk provides a loose jusification for government efforts to ease the transitional burdens that sudden alterations in policy instruments create.

As a practical matter it is hard to draw a line between central bank efforts to maintain aggregate liquidity by acting as lender of last resort and FDIC and FSLIC efforts to minimize deposit institution failures. However, a useful theoretetical principle may be enunciated. The Federal Reserve should hold itself responsible through the discount window for easing transitional problems caused by unpredictable shifts in its policy, but individual institutions should be held answerable for the extent of their exposure to the risk of interest volatility.

The major purpose of net worth accounts at deposit institutions is to help federal agencies to maintain confidence in these institutions'

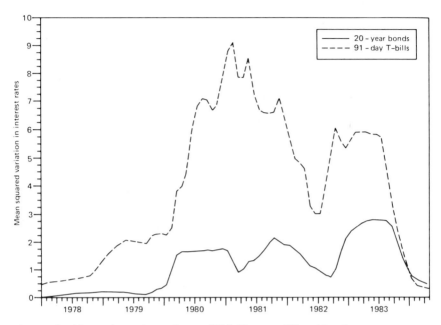

Figure 1.3 12-month moving variance of U.S. Treasury bill and bond rates

ability to cope with adversity: to buffer severe financial pressures that might emanate from instances of unfavorable economic conditions or employee misjudgment and crime. As long as deposit insurance guarantees remain both credible and underpriced, far too few deposit institution managers find the benefits of strengthening their capital accounts to be worth the cost of raising additional equity (Buser, Chen, and Kane 1981). Systematically underpricing deposit insurance has induced a massive and ongoing substitution of equity in the form of deposit insurance guarantees for private equity in deposit institutions. The federal government is already the leading supplier of equity funds to deposit institutions. The problem is not that deposit institutions have been doing more business than can be supported by their capital accounts but that the composition and funding of deposit institution capital accounts have shifted uncontrollably. To reverse the process, federal deposit insurance coverages and pricing policies must be reformed. For deposit institutions to remain part of the private sector, incentives to invest private capital in deposit institutions must be restored.

4. *Outlook for deposit insurance reform*

During the 1970s economists continued to call for risk-rated deposit insurance premiums (Scott and Mayer 1971; Gibson 1972; Merton 1978; McCulloch 1981) and for changes in coverage (Mayer 1975; Silverberg and Flechsig 1978). In the early 1980s the heads of both the FDIC and the FSLIC finally acknowledged the need for their agencies to develop a system of risk-rated premiums. In October 1982 Congress asked the deposit insurance agencies to study the feasibility of extending their coverage of deposits and the possibility of allowing private insurance and reinsurance for this coverage. During the next six months FDIC Chairman William Isaac opened a public dialogue concerning ways to overhaul the deposit insurance system. While campaigning for increasing the strength of implicit premiums through greater disclosure, he proposed putting large depositors more at risk in bank failures, encouraging private insurance companies to underwrite some deposit insurance risks, and making bank examiners responsible for levying risk-related explicit premiums on individual institutions. He further proposed that the FSLIC be merged into the FDIC and that the supervisory functions of the various federal deposit institution regulators be consolidated into a single agency. His agency's staff-prepared report to the House banking committee (FDIC 1983) ultimately endorsed a series of reforms cautiously designed to implement these principles.

For its part the FHLBB, which controls the FSLIC, called for general comments on a loose plan to establish graduated premiums. In this plan surcharges for risk would raise charges for risky institutions by as much as 50 percent over the basic premium. It simultaneously engaged a panel of academic consultants as a drafting committee to help prepare its own congressionally mandated report (FHLBB 1983).

How the Need for Deposit Insurance Reform Aggravates Other Regulatory Problems

Although both agencies' reports emphasized the need for change and recommended bold action, the House and Senate banking committees so far have attached little urgency to deposit insurance reform. The entry of nondepository financial services firms into banking, the reciprocal entry of depository firms into nontraditional markets, the de facto spread of interstate banking, and the desirability of paying explicit interest on demand deposits and required reserves pushed the question of reforming deposit insurance off the effective legislative agenda. This is ironic in that the subsidies to risk-taking hidden in the current system of deposit insurance play a large role in making these other problems seem so very urgent. Without prior reform of the deposit insurance system, the nation's financial structure cannot be controlled effectively.

Any comprehensive solution to the deposit insurance mess must endeavor to restore market discipline. The FDIC and FSLIC must act more like private insurers so that uninsured depositors and stockholders bear more of the risk inherent in deposit institution operations. Opportunities for risky institutions to fail must be administratively unblocked (for example, by authorizing bailouts only when a fixed percentage of insured institutions has failed within the past twelve months) and timely disclosure of problem situations must be adopted. A useful first step would be the replacement of book value accounting for insured institutions by market value accounting. A second step would be to expand FDIC and FSLIC rights to supervise insured institutions and to cancel insurance coverage in timely fashion. Currently deposit insurers are required to phase out an institution's coverage over a two-year period and may not start this process until completing a time-consuming notification and hearings process. To rebalance insured institutions' own rights, opportunities for private competition in deposit insurance must be established. The easiest way to do this would be to lower the basic coverage from $100,000 to $10,000 per account name and, by indexing this coverage to a general price index, to remove this value from the legislative arena as far as possible.

Deposit institutions should be able to purchase supplementary coverage, perhaps in $10,000 layers, from either federal or private insurers. At the same time individual account holders should be able to purchase additional insurance for their accounts from private companies. To make sure that private institutions have a legitimate opportunity to compete for layers of secondary coverage, the FDIC and FSLIC should be required to hold periodic auctions for insurance companies to bid on opportunities to reinsure these contracts. Finally, to keep expectations from developing that private deposit insurance carriers will themselves be routinely bailed out whenever deposit institution failures push any of them to the brink of insolvency, government assistance of these companies should be legislatively constrained.

So far, although the Treasury has been drafting a parallel plan, the FSLIC's plan and reform proposals floated by the FDIC exist as trial balloons developed for submission to Congress. Neither agency has irreversibly committed itself to undertaking fundamental reform. The agencies' public dialogue continues to duck the three basic questions of risk management: (1) How comprehensively should client portfolio risk be conceived? (2) How accurately and how regularly should this risk be measured? (3) What degree of graduation in the premium schedule would be sufficiently steep to eliminate the subsidy to risk-bearing? Until the full resources of the deposit insurance bureaucracy are mobilized to make the development of an operational plan a number-one priority, resolution of these issues figures to be stymied by political tensions endemic to the legislative process, to the bureaucratic structure of regulatory agencies, and to regulator-regulatee relationships.

Congressional Denial of the Need for Deposit Insurance Reform

Although great progress has been made since 1982, the essentially political impasse causes great distress to many academic economists. Congressional committees' skeptical attitude toward testimony about the need for federal deposit insurance reform reminds me of a country doctor whose wife developed a serious heart condition. Because his town had not yet been wired for telephone service, he rigged up a large bell that his children could ring to alert him if his wife's condition should require his attention while he was off treating other patients. Soon after he installed this emergency warning system, the children rang the bell frantically just as he was concluding his first call of the day. Leaping into his buggy and whipping his horse into a near-frenzy, he raced home in record time. Dashing up to his wife's bedroom, he was told that she had suffered some slight shortness of breath and mild chest pain, but that her difficulties had passed when she lay down. When an extremely cursory examination uncovered no compelling reason for alarm, he scolded the children for diverting him from his rounds and for subjecting him and his horse to such unnecessary stress. Then, he left for his second call.

As he completed treating the second patient, the bell rang out anew. Again, the doctor dashed home, nearly killing his horse in the process. Reaching the house, he virtually flew up the stairs and rushed gasping into his wife's bedroom, where she was resting peacefully and talking with the children. The children explained that, although she had felt intense chest and arm pains for several minutes, the pains had stopped when they gave her some digitalis. In a state of great aggravation, he brought the children outside the room and lectured them even more sternly about the value of his services to the rest of the community and the importance of calling him only when a real problem existed.

However, he didn't even reach the location of his third patient before the bell rang out once more. Spurred on by the unhappy fate of the boy who cried wolf, he drove back as fast as he could. As he rushed up the porch and into the house, his horse keeled over dead behind him. This time, when the doctor reached his wife's bedroom, she was rolling on the floor in severe pain, turning blue, and gasping desperately for breath. Beaming approvingly on the children, he proclaimed, "Now, *that's* more like it."

Using an antiquated system for developing and communicating information, deposit insurance officials have been trying to tell a preoccupied Congress some bad news about the financial health of deposit institutions. Despite conducting a succession of committee hearings on the subject, Congress has chosen repeatedly to close its ears to this news. Ironically, if an undeniable deposit insurance crisis were to occur, far from acknowledging the timeliness and correctness of the regulators' repeated warnings, Congress would spank its children and rebuke them publicly for having failed previously to make the extent of the developing danger sufficiently clear. In refusing to act on the warnings of these officials, Congress is forfeiting the chance to institute reforms that could forestall the bureaucratic crisis that continued inattention to the problem may force on us.

References and Additional Readings

Aspinwall, Richard. 1975. "Discussion." *Journal of Financial and Quantitative Analysis* 10 (November): 589–610.

Benston, George, and Pierce, James. 1981. "Discussions." In Karl Brunner, ed., *The Great Depression Revisited*. Boston: Martinus Nijhoff.

Burns, Helen M. 1974. *The American Banking Community and New Deal Banking Reforms, 1933–1935*. Contributions in Economics and Economic History, No. 11. Westport, Conn.: Greenwood Press.

Buser, Stephen A.; Chen, Andrew H.; and Kane, Edward J. 1981. "Federal Deposit Insurance, Regulatory Policy, and Optimal Bank Capital." *Journal of Finance* 35 (March): 51–60.

Emerson, Guy. 1934. "Guaranty of Deposits under the Banking Act of 1933." *Quarterly Journal of Economics* 48 (February): 229–244.

Federal Deposit Insurance Corporation. Various years. *Annual Report*. Washington, D.C.

Federal Deposit Insurance Corporation. 1983. *Deposit Insurance in a Changing Environment*, Washington, D.C., April 15.

Federal Home Loan Bank Board. 1983. *Agenda for Reform*. Washington, D.C., March 23.

Gibson, William E. 1972. "Deposit Insurance in the United States: Evaluation and Reform." *Journal of Financial and Quantitative Analysis* 7 (March): 1575–1594.

Golembe, Carter H. 1960. "The Deposit Insurance Legislation of 1933: An Examination of Its Antecedents and Its Purposes." *Political Science Quarterly* 75 (June): 181–200.

Green, George D. 1981. "The Ideological Origins of the Revolution in American Financial Policies." In Karl Brunner, ed., *The Great Depression Revisited*, pp. 220–252. Boston: Martinus Nijhoff.

Guttentag, Jack. 1984. "A Note on Hedging and Solvency: The Case of a Phoenix." *Journal of Futures Markets* 3 (Summer): 137–141.

Horvitz, Paul M. 1975. "Failures of Large Banks: Implications for Deposit Insurance and Banking Supervision." *Journal of Financial and Quantitative Analysis* 10 (November): 589–601.

Humphrey, David B. 1976. "100% Deposit Insurance: What Would It Cost?" *Journal of Bank Research* (Autumn): 192–198.

Kareken, John, and Wallace, Neil. 1978. "Deposit Insurance and Bank Regulation: A Partial Equilibrium Exposition." *Journal of Business* 51 (July): 413–438.

Klebaner, Benjamin J. 1974. *Commercial Banking in the United States: A History*. Hinsdale, Ill.: Dryden Press.

Kreps, Clifton, and Wacht, R. F. 1971. "A More Constructive Role for Deposit Insurance." *Journal of Finance* 26 (May): 605–613.

Leff, Gary. 1976. "Should Federal Deposit Insurance Be 100%?" *Bankers Magazine* 159 (Summer): 23–30.

Leff, Gary, and Park, J. W. 1977. "The Mississippi Deposit Insurance Crisis." *Bankers Magazine* 160 (Summer): 74–80.

McCulloch, J. Huston. 1981. "Interest Rate Risk and Capital Adequacy for Traditional Banks and Financial Intermediaries." In Sherman J. Maisel, ed., *Risk and Capital Adequacy in Commercial Banks*, pp. 223–248. National Bureau of Economic Research Monograph. Chicago: University of Chicago Press.

Mayer, Thomas. 1965. "A Graduated Deposit Insurance Plan." *Review of Economics and Statistics* 47 (February): 114–116.

Mayer, Thomas. 1975. "Should Large Banks Be Allowed to Fail?" *Journal of Financial and Quantitative Analysis* 10 (November): 603–613.

Mayers, David, and Smith, Clifford L., Jr. 1982. *Toward a Positive Theory of Insurance*. Monograph Series in Finance and Economics. New York: Graduate School of Business Administration, New York University.

Merton, Robert C. 1978. "On the Cost of Deposit Insurance When There Are Surveillance Costs." *Journal of Business* 51 (July): 439–452.

Rosenberg, Barr, and Perry, Philip R. 1978. "The Fundamental Determinants of Risk in Banking." In *Proceedings from a Conference on Bank Structure and Competition*, pp. 402–477. Chicago: Federal Reserve Bank of Chicago.

Scott, Kenneth W., and Mayer, Thomas. 1971. "Risk and Regulation in Banking: Some Proposals for Deposit Insurance." *Stanford Law Review* 23 (May): 857–902.

Silverberg, Stanley C., and Flechsig, Theodore G. 1978. "The Case for 100% Insurance of Demand Deposits." *Issues in Bank Regulation* 1 (Winter): 38–44.

Sinkey, Joseph F., Jr. 1979. *Problem and Failed Institutions in the Commercial Banking Industry*. Greenwich, Conn.: JAI Press.

Sinkey, Joseph F., Jr. 1985. "Regulatory Attitudes toward Risk." In Richard C. Aspinwall and Robert S. Eisenbeis, eds., *The Banking Handbook*, pp. 347–380. New York: Wiley.

Spong, Kenneth, and Hoenig, Thomas. 1979. "Bank Examiner Classifications and Loan Risk." *Economic Review*, Federal Reserve Bank of Kansas City (June): 15–25.

Chapter 2

Insolvency-Resolution Policies of the Deposit Insurance Agencies

Technically deposit insurance is misnamed. Rather than insuring deposits against a particular set of hazards, it places the credit standing of one of three federal agencies behind the deposit liabilities of an insured institution. In effect the deposit insurance agencies guarantee the first $100,000 of the deposit contracts their clients issue. A guarantee differs from insurance in that it is contingent on the nonfulfillment of designated provisions of a financial contract. At the same time a guarantor is different from a cosigner in that a guarantor's credit does not stand equally with that of the maker of the contract. Before the guarantor's pledge becomes collectible, the maker of the contract must suffer the consequences of failing to perform obligations under the contract.

Each of the three insurance agencies serves a segmented institutional clientele, although the degree of segmentation has been relaxed by the Garn–St Germain Depository Institutions Act of 1982. The FDIC insures deposit accounts of commercial banks, state-chartered mutual savings banks, and (since the 1982 act) any mutual savings bank that elects not to switch its insurer when converting to a federal charter. The FSLIC insures deposit accounts of S&Ls and a rapidly growing number of other federal savings banks. The National Credit Union Share Insurance Fund insures accounts held at credit unions.

These agencies may be viewed as subsidiaries of a vast federal holding company erected to insured U.S. citizens against a growing variety of economic hazards. Government-insured risks range today from the impoverishing effects of old age and ill health to casualty losses from natural disasters, foreign competition, and securities fraud (Aharoni 1981). Each subsidiary insurance agency has an economic and political history rooted in the interplay of interest group politics. This is because every subsidiary serves both to pool risks across exposed individuals and to shift a burden of unfunded sectoral risk onto the holding company (i.e., the body politic). In the case of deposit insurance, a March 1982 joint congressional resolution (House Congressional Resolution 290) places the "full faith and credit" of the U.S. government behind the subsidiaries' unfunded liabilities.

This book neglects the credit union fund and funds operated by various state-sponsored corporations to focus on identifying the unfunded burdens currently associated with the operations of the FDIC and FSLIC. Explicit premiums for this insurance are paid, in the first instance, by insured institutions. However, at least some of the net burden from this insurance (which could be in principle either a net cost or a net benefit) is ultimately shifted forward and backward to other parties by incorporating the net burden occasioned by deposit insurance into the prices faced by deposit institution customers and into the wages and salaries offered to managers and employees.

Why Insure Deposits and Depositors?

Deposit insurance agencies serve three wide-ranging and frequently contradictory public purposes. The overriding mission is to serve the president and the Congress as agents and shields. As agents the insurance agencies must adapt their policies to the larger economic programs of elected politicians. This goal makes them responsive to various political constituencies and puts them in the business of subsidizing designated financial activities and markets (such as mortgage lending by thrift institutions) even when such redistributive policies conflict somewhat with their strictly economic interest as deposit insurers. As shields their task is to protect elected politicians from public criticism. Whenever a scandal breaks involving unsafe or unsound banking practices, the insurance agencies and other deposit institution regulators must accept blame for not having nipped the problem in the bud.

Making it hard for deposit institutions to abuse their fiduciary responsibilities is part of the economic efficiency mission of deposit insurance. This activity aims at overcoming deposit institution managers' informational advantage over their customers. By undertaking to guarantee client deposits, the insurance agencies relieve account holders of moderate means of any need to worry about whether a deposit institution will meet its obligations to depositors. Guaranteeing client performance in deposit markets figuratively lets the FDIC and FSLIC stand in the shoes of depositors (Black, Miller, and Posner 1978). In representing and enforcing the beneficial interest of depositors as a class, the insurance agencies cooperate with chartering agencies and the Fed. Together they produce a public good—periodic examinations and continuous supervision—that allows depositors and overlapping regulators to conserve their own monitoring resources. Coordinating efforts to oversee client performance avoids the waste of duplicate monitoring efforts and reduces opportunities for institutions both to misrepresent their economic condition to depositors and to undertake projects that would exploit depositors' informational disadvantage. Since 1979 the federal examination effort has been overseen by the interagency Federal Financial Institutions Examination Council (FFIEC).

Alongside its redistributive and economic efficiency purposes, deposit insurance has a macroeconomic goal: to avoid destructive swings in public confidence as to the redeemability of deposit instruments. As a practical matter this goal is pursued by preventing individual deposit institution failures from cumulating to levels that would alarm the public.

Each insurance agency shares the responsibility with the Federal Reserve System for promoting these goals and for stabilizing financial markets. As the nation's central bank, the Fed is charged with guarding the stability of the payments system in general and of the money supply in particular. Microeconomic responsibilities are shared in even finer measure with the Office of the Comptroller of the Currency (which charters national banks) and with state banking departments (which supervise the entry and exit of state-chartered institutions). Within the FFIEC on particular supervisory issues, the bureaucratic interests of the Fed and the Comptroller can easily run counter to those of the insurance agencies.

Multiple goals and a system of multiply shared responsibility for their achievement is a sure formula for practical conflict. Across the business cycle the major recurring conflict occurs between short-run benefits from avoiding deposit institution failures by adopting policies that bail out troubled clients on a needs basis as against the long-run effects of such policies on risk-bearing incentives. A policy of bailing out notoriously insolvent institutions rather than closing them and taking over their assets undermines the discipline of the market. When investors perceive the odds to be good that potential losses will be truncated by government assistance, prospective payoffs from pursuing spectacular risks are enhanced.

Deposit Insurance Coverages

FDIC and FSLIC insurance is mandatory for federally chartered institutions, for state-chartered members of the Federal Reserve System, and, by the decision of individual state legislatures, for nongrandfathered state-chartered institutions in most states. (Grandfathering is the practice of exempting various existing institutions from some or all of the effects of a new law.) Even though explicit premiums are expressed as a percentage (1/12 of 1 percent) of a client's total deposits at domestic offices, FDIC and FSLIC guarantees cover only a portion of these liabilities. Very large depositors are left formally uninsured on the hypothesis that substantial depositors should be able to look out for themselves. At least initially deposit insurance was conceived as a scheme for protecting small depositors. Today FDIC and FSLIC coverage applies formally to the first $100,000 (raised over time from $2,500 in 1933) in each depositor's accounts at the domestic offices of an insured institution. An individual can multiply this effective coverage almost without limit by opening accounts in joint names or in a number of insured institutions. In fact deposit brokerage firms have developed that employ computer software and telecommunications to split large balances advantageously across different institutions without exceeding the $100,000 limit at any single depository.

Formally insurance does not apply at all to deposits booked at foreign branches and to nondeposit liabilities such as federal funds (claims to balances on the books of the Federal Reserve that are purchased temporarily from another financial institution), securities repurchase agreements, or contracts executed in the futures markets. Because the average size of deposit accounts tends to rise with an institution's total assets, the percentage of insured deposits tends to be lower for large institutions than for small ones. At the same time the substitution of deposits in foreign branches and of nondeposit liabilities for domestic deposits also tends to rise with institutional size and with the level of market interest rates as well. Hence, calculated as a percentage of total assets or as a percentage of nonequity liabilities, a bank's proportionate insurance premium declines with an institution's asset size. Given FDIC and FSLIC reluctance to kill off large institutions, this means that, relative to smaller firms and especially when interest rates are high, large banks and thrifts pay too little rather than too much for the guarantees they receive. As one way to lessen this problem, in August 1984 Senator William Proxmire introduced a bill to require that U.S. banks pay insurance premiums on their foreign deposits.

Liquidity Shortages, Runs, and Book Value Insolvency

For an insured institution deposit insurance moderates three escalating types of potential shortage. The least serious difficulty consists of temporary shortages of liquidity that confront any deposit institution at one time or another. Such shortages occur whenever an institution's cash, reserve balances, and established lines of credit prove insufficient to accommodate comfortably an unanticipated and transitory imbalance in the inflow and outflow of customer funds. At such times contemporary depository institutions typically purchase liquidity by issuing uninsured short-term liabilities. Because deposit insurance augments the credit standing of client institutions, it makes transitory strains on an institution's liquidity easier to manage than they would otherwise be.

When a liquidity shortage continues long enough to require a restructuring of an institution's balance sheet, the need for more equity or longer-term outside borrowing becomes intense. To relieve such problems, deposit insurance agencies themselves may provide credit on advantageous terms or may assist a troubled client to borrow from the Fed or, when the client is an S&L, from its regional FHLB.

If an ongoing liquidity shortage is not relieved by outside borrowing, assets may have to be sold for less than full value. Such sales erode an institution's capital position. In turn, observed declines in net worth may spook an intitution's uninsured creditors by creating doubt about the institution's ability to repay its debts. When uninsured customers move their funds en masse to safer locations, they create a run on a bank's resources. In the 1930s a run was signaled by worried depositors lining up in great numbers outside an institution's offices. Today a run centers on access to nondeposit liabilities such as federal funds and repurchase agreements and on the behavior of large depositors (especially foreign ones). Modern depositors may electronically disburse the uninsured portion of their checking and savings balances, and as featured in the financial-horror film, *Rollover*, refuse to renew holdings of maturing large denomination certificates of deposit (CDs).

To meet a run, an institution must borrow nondeposit funds or sell earning assets. Occasionally a run is arrested by strong credit support from a financial institution with which it has a correspondent relationship. However, because an institution that is under pressure seldom shapes up as an attractive credit to private lenders, borrowed funds typically come from government sources. Unlike borrowings, asset sales tend to push the book value of an institution's assets toward their market value. Given that deposit runs typically are provoked by the presence of sizable unrealized losses in an institution's balance sheet, asset sales tend to push a troubled firm toward what is called technical or book value insolvency. Book value insolvency occurs when the book value of an institution's net worth accounts (i.e., the difference between the book values of its assets and liabilities) crosses over into negative values. Of course book value insolvency may develop without a prior run. This tends to occur in either of two ways. On rare occasions a scheduled government examination of an institution's books may uncover evidence that a substantial decline in net worth has occurred since the previous examination. Such a decline typically reflects employee theft, malfeasance, or sudden losses on loans or in foreign exchange, futures, or forward transactions. Alternatively, after a period of governmental assistance meant to stave off book value insolvency, the client's deposit insurance agency may decide it is in its bureaucratic interest to ask the chartering agency to revoke the firm's charter and certify the firm's insolvency by acknowledging that various still-unbooked losses are imminent.

Procedures for Managing Deposit Institution Insolvencies

Next to their pricing policies, the most questionable aspect of FDIC and FSLIC operations is their strategy for preventing and handling individual deposit institution insolvencies. These policies may be likened to medical triage (pronounced "tree-ahje"), the process by which doctors in a battlefield or disaster situation decide which of the many casualties strung out before them are too far gone to send into surgery. Triage seeks to apportion limited therapeutic resources across casualties according to their capacity for ultimate recovery and the immediacy of their need for intervention. Treating deposit institution casualties equally lessens immediate political frictions visited on the insurance agencies, but it wastes agency resources. It is hard to justify a policy of financing the continued financial play of institutions whose prospects are poor. Lacking the deep pockets of a government agency, a private insurer would insist that a troubled firm rebuild its capital on its own, locate a voluntary merger partner, or turn its operation over to the insurer.

Reflecting the conflict between their macroeconomic and microeconomic responsibilities, the insurance agencies show a de facto commitment to minimizing the risks of cumulative failures that surpass their de jure commitment to safe and sound banking. Their policy of systematically delaying a troubled institution's formal demise until the last possible moment gives sophisticated and knowledgeable uninsured creditors an advantage relative to other uninsured parties and to the FDIC and FSLIC as well. Although postponing de jure failure avoids closings in some cases, it always gives uninsured creditors time to improve their position. Other things equal, this tends to increase the cost to the insurance agencies of resolving the specific failures that do occur. However, keeping a troubled institution open also gives it access to low-rate credit through the Fed's discount window. De facto subsidies inherent in these loans transfer some of the costs to another set of federal pockets.

As soon as a bank is suspected of being in danger of failure, uninsured creditors have an incentive to secure their position against the possibility of liquidation. The most straightforward ways to do this are by moving (in the case of demand deposit customers) checking account funds to other institutions, by selling off other liabilities to less-aware parties, or by converting them to cash at the first opportunity. But uninsured creditors may improve their position in other less obvious ways, in particular by taking out loans that in the event of liquidation legally offset their holdings of uninsured deposits. (Under federal bankruptcy law a depositor's right to offset outstanding loans against unpaid deposit claims is not absolute. However, applicable state law and deposit insurance practice generally put a depositor-borrower in a stronger position than a mere depositor.) It may also be possible to negotiate priority in collection or pledges of specific collateral for the debt instruments they hold. In the long-delayed Franklin National Bank failure in 1974, about three-fourths of uninsured demand deposits and one-third of uninsured deposits of all kinds turned out to be protected by loan offsets (Barnett, Horvitz, and Silverberg 1977, p. 313).

On the other hand, delaying failure creates no incentives for insured depositors to adjust their accounts. The passivity of insured depositors reduces the number of cases that need to be resolved by paying off insured deposits and subsequently liquidating the institution's assets. Deposit payoffs kill the corporation, extinguishing the relationships of established loan and deposit customers and disturbing local economies by putting an institution's offices out of operation. They also cause loan collection costs for the insurance agency and introduce potentially protracted delays in settling uninsured creditors' claims against the assets of the failed institution. A deposit institution is generally more valuable to an acquirer when it is taken alive rather than dead, at least when payments under executive separation contracts are not excessive and as long as the insurance agency agrees to indemnify the acquirer against still-undiscovered losses. This is because a live bank acquisition preserves the right to carry the failing firm's past losses forward against future taxes and because the assets of a going concern include ongoing customer relationships that dissipate quickly once an institution is closed. However, the preservation of tax loss carryforwards produces no value for the government as a whole. It merely shifts the cost of resolving the failure from the books of the FDIC to those of the Treasury. Moreover, killing the institution should save some resources by rendering the firm's management contracts and various debt obligations unenforceable.

Whatever the balance of economic pros and cons, the dominant reasons for the FDIC's and FSLIC's revealed dispreference for deposit payoffs, especially as a method for resolving the failure of a large institution, appear to be political and bureaucratic. First, the agencies appear overly concerned with avoiding negative cash flows in the year the failure is resolved. Second, they seem to fear the political consequences of imposing on individual customers the adjustment costs of searching out new deposit institution relationships. Finally, payoffs increase the chance of disrupting the public's confidence in other deposit institutions that may own uninsured deposits in the failed institution or have made loans to it.

Four methods exist for resolving a potential failure without a deposit payoff: (1) direct assistance, which usually means making a subsidized loan to (or taking an explicit equity position in) a troubled institution; (2) reorganization, which involves a concessionary restructuring of the institution's uninsured debt; (3) interim FSLIC or FDIC operation of a failed institution; and (4) financially assisted purchase-and-assumption transactions.

Although 1982 legislation temporarily expands opportunities for providing direct assistance to troubled institutions, in practice the preeminent approach for resolving client failures used by the FDIC and FSLIC is to arrange a purchase-and-assumption transaction, with deposit payoff itself running a distant second. In the past direct assistance has been used more frequently by the FSLIC than by the FDIC. Before the interest rate turnaround of 1982, direct assistance had seldom returned an assisted institution to de facto solvency. Even if it were a consistently successful method for reviving a moribund firm, direct assistance has inappropriate effects on future incentives in that it benefits the stockholders and/or managers that brought the institution into the state of needing assistance.

As a result of the decline in market interest rates experienced in the last half of 1982 and most of 1983, the three-year program of capital assistance mandated by the Garn–St Germain Depository Institutions

Act of 1982 has proved much less significant than it looked when it was first proposed. In late 1982 combined FDIC and FSLIC projections held that roughly $2.1 billion in program aid would be outstanding in 1985. By year-end 1982 the FDIC had already distributed $174.5 million of assistance to fifteen savings banks. However, partly because of paperwork and differential eligibility requirements, the FSLIC program developed far more modestly than originally anticipated. At year-end 1983 the FSLIC held only $77.2 million of these certificates, and even by midyear 1984, only eighty associations had participated in the FSLIC program. In any case the kind of aid provided is little more than an accounting trick. Moreover, it is made available only to nonaggressively managed clients that have experienced losses in the preceding two quarters and whose recorded net worth has slipped below 3 percent of their assets. The FDIC and FSLIC merely swap their promissory notes for obligations called "net worth certificates" that are issued by eligible clients. Since the securities swapped both pay the same yield, only in the sense that regulators arbitrarily agree to count their own promissory notes to the insurance agency as client capital do net worth ratios improve for assisted firms. Moreover, this largely paper improvement in client balance sheets further increases the government's equity stake in assisted institutions. It moves the industry one step closer to de facto nationalization.

Reorganizing troubled institutions is seldom a practical option because restructuring is hard to effect without open negotiations with creditors that call attention to the institution's weakened condition and threaten to bring on a panicky flight of uninsured deposits. On the other hand insurance agency operation of an insolvent firm is hard to justify for more than a limited span of time. Moreover, unlike the FSLIC's freedom to operate phoenix institutions, the FDIC may operate a deposit insurance bank only when the services of the institution are deemed "essential" to its local community. This determination is fundamentally a political one that turns on the clout of the constituencies the institution serves. Under current law, when the FDIC chooses this option, it has a maximum of two years either to transfer the bank's business to another firm or to close out the bank's operations. In practice the FDIC resorts to this solution for political reasons when it proves hard in timely fashion to locate or to indemnify an acceptable takeover candidate.

All this serves to explain agency preferences for purchase-and-assumption transactions. In a purchase-and-assumption transaction, the insurer solicits bids for the failing institution as a going concern. Typically a stronger institution purchases at auction some or all of the failing institution's assets and assumes all of its deposits. When an institution is purchased without first being declared insolvent and formally closed, the merger is termed an open-bank acquisition, and the acquiring firm automatically assumes the institution's nondeposit liabilities as well. Whatever assets are not purchased are retained by the insurance agency in its corporate capacity. In the event of a closed-bank acquisition the seller is the insurance agency itself, which upon the bank's closing becomes the receiver for its affairs. In a nonmutual institution receivership takes control away from stockholders as well as managers; however, a receiver has to respect court-imposed standards of fairness. Recent case law suggests that even in a closed-bank transaction, the claims of all nonsubordinated creditors have to be accorded equal priority. Although the insurance agencies would like the courts to regard a failed institution's insured deposits as having a preference in liquidation over its uninsured liabilities, it is doubtful that uninsured deposits and nondeposit liabilities may be reduced to residual claims against the assets the insurance agency retains without congressional action or prior incorporation of specific contract language to this effect (Brooks and Vartanian 1982).

An inventive technique for subordinating uninsured creditors to insured depositors without violating the principle of equality in liquidation was first used by the FSLIC in 1982 and by the FDIC in 1983. Dubbed a deposit transfer, it is best conceived as an indirect payoff. This hybrid method provides for a full payoff of insured depositors and a partial payoff of uninsured accounts through the agency of an acquiring bank that assumes the liability for administering the deposits that are transferred. The technique is a closed-bank transaction, whose distinguishing feature is that the insurance agency accepts bids only for the sum of the insured deposits and that portion of the uninsured deposits the agency believes that it will recover in liquidating the failed institution.

Although the insurance agency simultaneously leases some or all of the failed institution's office locations to the acquirer, the agency retains all other uninsured liabilities and all assets in a liquidation account. If the legality of the subordination arrangement implicit in this scheme is affirmed by the courts, more frequent use of this method of failure resolution can increase the effective risk exposure of uninsured creditors in deposit institution failures.

When the failed institution's assets and liabilites are acquired in toto, a purchase-and-assumption transaction reduces to a simple takeover or merger. It is useful to distinguish between voluntary and supervisory mergers. Supervisory mergers are instigated by a specific insurance agency search for takeover bids. In a supervisory merger the insurance agency typically provides financial assistance to the acquiring institution. In such transactions *assistance* is a euphemistic term for compensation required to balance the deal. This compensation fills in the gap between the market value of the liabilities an acquirer assumes and the market value of the bookable and unbookable assets being transferred with them. Until recently agency assistance took the form of cash payments to the acquirer. Since 1981 assistance has frequently taken the form of promissory notes that obligate the insurance agency involved to make a stream of future payments. When some or all of the promised payments are contingent on the future performance of the assets acquired, the note is called an income-maintenance agreement. The capitalized value of agency obligations in these agreements cannot properly be calculated by conventional present value formulas employing consensus forecasts of future interest rates. The market value of an income-maintenance agreement includes an additional premium for the interest volatility risk impounded in the contingent guarantee. To price contingency elements, economists have developed option pricing analysis.

The amount of assistance required to finance a takeover is determined by the difference between the market values, not the book values, of the acquired institution's assets and liabilities. After marking bookable assets to their current market value, whatever gap in book value is not filled in by insurance agency assistance is called the *purchase premium* and accounted as goodwill. It represents an auction-derived estimate of the value of unbookable assets in the acquired firm's operation. This regulator-approved accounting approach is termed *purchase accounting*. To illustrate how it works, let us suppose that the acquirer of an insolvent bank purchases loans and physical capital (which are recognized as bookable assets) from the acquired bank valued at $4 million and assumes $10 million worth of its liabilities. If the acquirer negotiates only $5 million in cash assistance from the FDIC, the acquirer would be said to have paid $5 million for the combination of bookable and unbookable assets it purchased. The $1 million premium over the market value of the bookable assets acquired is treated as a payment made to purchase undesignated unbookable assets such as the right to enjoy deposit insurance guarantees on the ongoing customer relationships of the absorbed institution. The premium is recorded in a good-will account that must be depreciated over the next ten to fifteen years.

In FDIC parlance when (after deducting the purchase premium) the agency replaces a failing bank's substandard assets with cash, notes, or insurance agency indemnifications, the acquirer is said to purchase a *clean bank*. Clean-bank transactions typically occur when evaluating the quality of some assets of the failing firm promises to prove extremely time-consuming or when some of the firm's contingent liabilities are difficult to document.

Purchase-and-assumption transactions are difficult to negotiate in unit banking states where for antitrust reasons nearby banks may not qualify as acceptable takeover candidates or when (as in the failure of the Penn Square Bank) poor or dishonest record keeping makes it impossible to document the extent of the institution's contingent liabilities on the closing date. To overcome the latter condition, the FDIC occasionally has promised to indemnify an acquiring institution against undocumented claims. But because this solution exposes agency resources to what are open-ended and avoidable risks, indemnification is rarely used.

When the market value of thrift institution net worth plummeted in the early 1980s, federal banking regulators' reluctance to approve interstate and interinstitutional mergers of distressed thrifts sharply limited the pool of potential bidders for the franchises of failing institutions. Because the resulting restrictions tended to reduce the average value of winning bids, they increased the pressure on FDIC and FSLIC insurance reserves. To relieve this pressure, federal authorities pragmatically began to relax these restrictions in supervisory mergers and acquisitions, especially (under the leadership of the FSLIC) the policy against interstate acquisitions. Such transactions may be interpreted as tied sales of regulatory exemptions and failing institutions. The sales are tied because the exemptions are not otherwise for sale.

Beginning in December 1981 interstate and cross-industry acquisitions of failing thrift institutions were approved in special circumstances. The number of such cases has grown rapidly. In 1982 the FSLIC approved eleven interstate mergers and two interstate holding company acquisitions, and the FDIC approved two intrastate cross-industry commercial bank acquisitions of thrifts. The Depository Institutions Act of 1982 (which was not signed into law until October 1982) routinizes interstate bidding and codifies the range of relevant circumstances and the set of potential acquirers from which the FDIC and FSLIC may solicit bids. It specifically authorizes federal regulators to consider takeover bids for failing institutions according to the following schedule of priorities: (1) from depository institutions of the same type within the same state, (2) from depository institutions of the same type in different states, (3) from depository institutions of different types in the same state, and (4) from depository institutions of different types in different states.

In considering offers from different states, the law requires federal regulators to give priority to offers from adjoining states. Special provisions for handling the failure of institutions with $500 million or more in assets received their first test during the weekend of February 12 and 13, 1983, when eight banks (including Atlanta's Citizens & Southern National Bank and a North Carolina bank holding company) bid for the United American Bank of Knoxville, Tennessee, in a closed-bank transaction. Although the out-of-state institutions outbid everyone else in the first round of bidding, the eventual in-state winner (First Tennessee National Corp.) was invited to participate in a second round of negotiations because its initial offer had been within 15 percent of the highest bid received. The largest interstate acquisition was Bank of America's takeover of the ailing Seattle-based Seafirst Corporation in July 1983.

Table 2.1 Balance sheet of assets and liabilities that FDIC and FSLIC may convey to an acquirer in a purchase-and-assumption transaction

Assets	Liabilities
Financial assets of a failing bank	**Deposits**
Clean assets	Insured
Dirty assets	Uninsured
Physical assets of a failing bank	**Documentable nondeposit liabilities**
Plant and equipment	Unsubordinated debt
Wholly owned subsidiaries	Subordinated debt
	Residual claims of shareholders against proceeds from asset liquidation
Commitments from the deposit insurance agency	**Undisclosed Liabilities**
Guarantees of insured deposits	
Indemnifications for undisclosed liabilities	
Income-maintenance agreements	
Regulatory exemptions	
From antitrust restrictions against intrastate mergers and acquisitions	
From restrictions against interstate mergers and acquisitions	
From restrictions against cross-industry acquisitions	

Note: Dirty assets and undisclosed liabilities represent items whose ultimate values are extraordinarily uncertain. The high variance of returns on these assets may make them too risky for some acquirers.

Determining the Costs and Benefits of Alternative Ways to Resolve a Failure

Table 2.1 summarizes the augmented balance sheet of asset and liability items that deposit insurance agencies may deploy to resolve a deposit institution failure. In principle FDIC and FSLIC officials are prepared to apportion these elements between themselves and one or more potential acquirers in whatever combination proves least costly overall to the deposit insurance fund. Hence the bidding process includes negotiations about which items ought and ought not to be conveyed in the final transaction.

Prior to the 1980s, in deciding between deposit payoffs and purchase-and-assumption transactions, officials did not explicitly review the possibility of granting income-maintenance agreements or permitting exemptions from restrictions against interstate and cross-industry takeovers. Moreover insured deposits were not conveyed differentially from uninsured ones (as they are in a deposit transfer—for example, in Seaway National's July 1983 takeover of the Union National Bank of Chicago), nor were an institution's deposit liabilities and branch office network broken up and sold in fragments to different acquirers (as they were, for example, in the February 1983 failure of American City Bank in Los Angeles). The discovery of these and several other unconventional ways of resolving a deposit institution failure resulted from the pressure of financial necessity. To stay solvent in the face of 1981–1984 demands on their resources, deposit insurance agencies had to expand their effective net worth far beyond the dollar value of their explicit insurance reserves.

In deciding how to resolve an individual failure, the deposit insurance agencies purport to choose the particular method that, given operative constraints on eligible bidders, involves the minimum cost to their insurance fund. However, the agencies retain much more latitude than this criterion would suggest. The cost of liquidating an institution is calculated as the sum of two items: the estimated discount between the book and market value of an institution's assets and the estimated costs of executing the liquidation. How to calculate the costs of alternative methods of failure resolution in particular cases is left to the discretion of the agency involved. Nor do the agencies report their methods for estimating the costs of alternative approaches in sufficient detail to let an external critic reproduce their alternative estimates. It is hard to believe that a strictly economic accounting of opportunity costs would have let deposit payoffs emerge as the favored vehicle only when a failed bank is either relatively small or its records are too messy to permit a reliable estimate of the bank's true liabilities.

Conjectural Guarantees Implicit in Agencies' Preferences for Purchase-and-Assumption Transactions

One cannot quarrel with the principle that the FDIC and FSLIC should strive to minimize the costs of failure resolution. But one can quarrel with the narrow conception of these costs that the FDIC and FSLIC currently employ. The cost that should be minimized is the sum of the direct and indirect costs of the decisions being made.

FDIC and FSLIC preference for arranging purchase-and-assumption transactions extends an implicit government blessing not only to uninsured deposits but also to nondeposit debt and to affiliated corporations of all sorts. During the time in which open bank takeover bids are solicited, uninsured creditors can and do improve their contingent postliquidation position at the expense of the insurance fund. This is particularly true for demand deposit and passbook customers who, by moving their funds to a safer haven, have at their own initiative the power to perfect a 100 percent de facto guarantee. The position of term depositors is only slightly less favorable since they may protect their position with loans and may expect to come out whole in either an open-bank or closed-bank purchase-and-assumption. Finally, in the event that an open-bank purchase-and-assumption is successfully negotiated, even holders of nondeposit debt are rescued.

As a result uninsured creditors of a troubled institution need concern themselves first with estimating the probability that the insolvency of a troubled institution will be resolved by a direct deposit payoff. Let us call this probability 1. Experience suggests that probability 1 is very low, especially for large institutions. Nondeposit creditors must also concern themselves with a second probability: the probability that even though a payoff is avoided, a closed-bank transaction will be negotiated that does not require the insurance agency or the acquiring institution to assume their liabilities. Let us call this probability 2. Experience and legal remedies available to disadvantaged creditors suggest that probability 2, though rising, is also very low and may be particularly low for institutions of very large size.

In an actuarial sense (which means when risks are weighted by probabilities suggested by experience), uninsured creditors of every insured institution conjecture that they possess nonnegligible implicit guarantees for the instruments they hold. The value of these implicit guarantees rises whenever information develops that makes probability 1 or 2 fall. Conversely the value of these guarantees falls whenever the flow of new information raises the odds that future settlements will be conducted in ways less favorable to uninsured parties than has been customary in the past.

Currently the FDIC and FSLIC express their determination to resolve deposit institution insolvencies by purchase-and-assumption transactions whenever this approach can be justified ex post. Actuarially this policy differs only slightly from a system that would administratively issue high-probability lottery tickets that, if validated, would provide full coverage to uninsured creditors. Some observers believe that the residual element of chance is unfair to the few unlucky deposit institution creditors whose tickets happen not to be drawn in the administrative lottery. Silverberg and Flechsig (1978) argue that because the lottery element generates customer efforts to shift large demand deposit balances out of troubled institutions, it produces pressure for hasty settlements that costs the insurance agencies more on average than the option not to redeem those accounts is worth. However, the skittishness of uninsured depositors makes aggressive bank managers more responsive to FDIC and FSLIC supervisory directives than they otherwise would be. Although the agencies can resort to civil sanctions such as cease and desist orders, their ability to spook uninsured depositors is these agencies' main source of clout in persuading individual clients to eliminate questionable management practices and to strengthen their balance sheets. Insulating demand deposits from the threat of unfavorable publicity would weaken the FDIC's and FSLIC's ability to restrict client risk-taking. If the consequences of unfavorable publicity were neutralized, one has to wonder whether clients would respond more than perfunctorily to agency pressure for changes in management practices or balance sheet structure.

A more telling objection to reliance on the purchase-and-assumption strategy is that it is systematically less workable for some types of institutions. The larger a troubled institution is and the more restrictive the branching laws under which this large bank operates, the more limited the set of potential acquirers with which the insurer may realistically negotiate an open-bank or closed-bank purchase. In turn the fewer the set of potential acquirers, the fewer chances an insurer has to sell a failing institution by auction and the more potential acquirers are encouraged to hold out for bargain terms. The tendency for acquirers to bargain stubbornly is reinforced by their knowledge that the larger the problem institution, the more its insurer will fear that liquidating it might trigger a run on weak institutions in other markets.

Protracted bargaining extends the time period over which uninsured creditors may make themselves whole. Some of them benefit passively as the passage of time brings their underwater claims to maturity at par, while others may use the time as a grace period in which to strengthen their positions against the possible onset of bankruptcy proceedings.

This asymmetry in the speed with which authorities can resolve the failures of large and small institutions puts uninsured creditors of very large institutions in possession of a more valuable set of implicit guarantees than that extended to creditors of smaller institutions. In effect large banks receive greater coverage than smaller banks do, even though all banks face the same structure of explicit premiums.

The inequity is underscored by the favorable treatment of uninsured creditors in the Continental Illinois case. To arrest a flight of uninsured creditors from the bank while it negotiated with potential acquirers, the FDIC in May 1984 arbitrarily extended its formal guarantee to all liabilities of the bank and its holding company. When negotiations broke down in July, all it had to gain from liquidating the bank was the possibility of absorbing the value of the stockholders' equity. Rather than straightforwardly nationalizing the bank, the FDIC and the Fed injected additional capital into the bank's balance sheet (partly in the form of the unbookable capitalized benefits of below-market Fed loans to Continental Illinois), and the FDIC took a large equity position that served to formalize the government's substantial ownership stake in the bank and left a substantial amount of stockholder funds behind on the bargaining table. On the day the FDIC resolution was announced, the market value of private stockholders' position in Continental Illinois closed at roughly $180 million.

An agency's decision not to enforce its de jure limitations on coverage in particular cases has long-run and system-wide costs that may outweigh the immediate economization of agency resources reputed to occur. It is myopic to calculate the costs of handling an individual insolvency as if the costs of resolving future insolvencies that matter are only those that occur in the very short run. Subsidies designed to arrest the cumulative short-run spread of current losses to a few other institutions undermine longer-run market sanctions against risk-bearing for all clients. Such a policy lowers the effective cost of deposit institution risk-bearing in ways that threaten to encourage surviving institutions to take even bolder risks in the future.

Innovations in Merger Assistance Policies

In the 1980s the FDIC and the FSLIC shifted away from assistance payments made entirely in cash to assistance packages executed at least partly in the form of promissory notes. Such notes are either interest-bearing securities or contingent obligations that guarantee a stream of future returns on the assets acquired. And in a number of cases, acquirers were granted valuable exemptions from rules against interstate operation or from antitrust strictures concerning the degree of concentration allowable in local deposit markets.

These policies were adopted to substitute implicit outlays for explicit outlays of agency funds. In contemporary thrift institution failures, the estimated present value of assistance committed is large relative to agency insurance funds. Providing merger assistance wholly in cash would have forced the FDIC and the FSLIC to show some of these outlays as an explicit decumulation of agency insurance reserves. Agency executives feared that booking these losses (which, properly accounted, should have approached the cost of liquidating the failed firms) would alarm uninsured creditors of client institutions and stimulate runs on troubled institutions.

FDIC Innovations

Without waiting for the agency's annual reports, one may determine the composition of FDIC merger assistance to a failing firm by examining agency press releases. Table 2.2 shows that the FDIC estimated that it provided over $1.8 billion in assistance payments to merging MSBs between 1981 and 1983. This figure (which is less than half the liquidation values recorded in the last column of the table) is roughly 15 percent of the FDIC insurance fund. Equivalently it is roughly the same as the agency's annual flow of interest and assessment income. Given

Table 2.2 Mutual savings banks involved in assisted mergers during 1981–1983 (dollar values in millions)

Bank	Date of merger	Estimated deposit size	FDIC disbursements reported in the next annual report	Composition of initial estimate							Estimated cost of deposit payoff
				Initial FDIC estimate of financial assistance provided	Cash or equivalent assets	Disadvantageous assumption of assets or loans	Income-maintenance agreement	FDIC notes	Unsubsidized loans	
Greenwich Savings Bank, New York City	Nov. 4, 1981	1,881	$ 437.5	$ 465.0	$100	$185	$180			$ 800
Central Savings Bank, New York City	Dec. 4, 1981	676	145.5	160.0	37.5	52.5	70			260
Union Dime Savings Bank, New York City	Dec. 18, 1981	1,172	2[a]	165.9	48.9		117			350
Western New York Savings Bank, Buffalo	Jan. 15, 1982	890	30.5	30.0	30.0					180
Farmers & Mechanics Savings Bank, Minneapolis	Feb. 21, 1982	789	86.2	95.0	30	15	50			250
United States Savings Bank, Newark	Mar. 12, 1982	578	69.4	65.0	11.4	25.6	28			168
Fidelity Mutual Savings Bank, Spokane	Mar. 15, 1982	551	81.5	47.0		8	15.7	23.3	30	165
New York Bank for Savings, New York City	Mar. 26, 1982	2,780	461.9	452.0	55		204	193		1,200
Western Savings Fund Society, Haverford, Penn.	April 3, 1982	1,957	425.5	294.0			182	112		696
United Mutual Savings Bank, New York City	Sept. 24, 1982	767	30.9	30.0				30		200
Mechanics Savings Bank, Elmira, N.Y.	Oct. 15, 1982	51	2.5	Negligible					2.5	6.9
Dry Dock Savings Bank, New York, N.Y.	Feb. 9, 1983	2,500	32.0	32.0			32.0			250[b]
Oregon Mutual Savings Bank, Portland, Oregon	Aug. 5, 1983	260	11.9	11.9	11.9					30.0
Auburn Savings Bank, Auburn, N.Y.	Oct. 1, 1983	130	2.9	2.9			2.9[b]		6.9[b]	18.0
Totals		14,982	1,818.2	1,850.7	324.7	286.1	881.6	358.3	39.4	4,573.9

Source: Selected FDIC press releases and information provided by FDIC staff members Stanley Silverberg and Pat Golodner.
a. Before the 1981 *Annual Report* was prepared, the Union Dime income-maintenance agreement had been folded into the assistance package for the New York Bank for Savings rescue. However, the figures reported for the New York Bank for Savings are understood to be net of this earlier commitment.
b. Estimates especially provided in 1984 by FDIC staff.

that commercial bank failures may have generated another several billion dollars in additional claims on FDIC resources (dominated by the Continental Illinois nationalization and the need to pay off depositors of the Penn Square Bank), a policy of payment in cash would have seriously depleted the FDIC's insurance fund. However, by making less than 20 percent of MSB assistance payments in cash and nearly eliminating rebates of assessment income to insured institutions, agency personnel managed to preserve the reported value of the insurance fund.

Some observers maintain that, on an actuarial basis, insurance premiums are excessive relative to realized losses and accumulated reserves (Miller 1981; Marcus and Shaked 1982). But the pace of technological change, insurance agencies' growing exposure to interest volatility risk (McCulloch 1983), and the pace and extent of innovation in FDIC and FSLIC insolvency-resolution policies suggest otherwise. One problem in conducting an actuarial analysis of FDIC and FSLIC cash flows is that fifty years of experience may not be long enough to produce a representative sample with respect to the frequency of severe crises. A second problem is that bureaucratic concern for establishing an appearance of good collection performance led to the use of accounting techniques that understated the losses suffered ex post in liquidating assets acquired in assisted mergers, nationalizations, and deposit payoff cases. By not including a charge for interest on agency funds tied up in uncollected assets, liquidation personnel made their efforts seem more productive than careful analysis would justify. Although this policy may have increased liquidators' sense of accomplishment, unaccounted interest must have encouraged them to hold on to interest-bearing assets until circumstances permitted them either to be sold or redeemed at par. Ironically overstating liquidators' collection success undermines the agency's ability to collect fair premiums. First, delaying the realization of losses postpones their impact on agency expenses and increases the value of interim rebates to clients. Second, it nowhere incorporates the capitalized value of the drain on future agency earnings this policy imposes. This feeds political pressure for even higher rebates and a lower insurance reserve.

Additional understatements of losses occur in FDIC calculations of the value of its income-maintenance agreements, which similarly neglect an important source of value. These instruments have been priced as if they offered a given stream of payments, determined by the obligations the agency would incur if future interest followed a particular projected path. These hypothetical payments are discounted at the FDIC's opportunity cost rate, which the FDIC considers to be roughly equivalent to the three-year Treasury yield. But this approach fails to account either for the interest subsidy that Treasury backing imparts to FDIC liabilities or to recognize the specifically contingent nature of the guarantees offered. The value of the contingency feature may be brought out by comparing these agreements to an option to buy a particular stock at any time in the next ten or fifteen years. This option gives the holder the right to benefit from any increase in the value of the stock without having to lose money if the stock price declines. The more volatile is the price of the underlying stock, the more valuable is this right. Similarly the value of FDIC income-maintenance agreements is a positive function of the volatility, as well as the expected mean of future interest rates.

Furthermore the cost of servicing these agreements should include an allowance for the costs of monitoring the takeover institution's performance of contractual obligations. These costs are particularly high for the Greenwich and Central agreements, which undertake to support earnings on the particular set of assets purchased for as long as these actually remain on the books of the acquiring institution. Other agreements still in force (the Union Dime agreement was rolled over into the guarantees negotiated in the takeover of the New York Bank for Savings) set up an artificial pool of assets to be supported, whose value in subsequent months is given by hypothetical paydown assumptions rather than by transactions in the specific assets acquired in the takeover. To complete negotiations aimed at putting the other two agreements on an artificially defined asset basis, the FDIC probably will have to grant additional concessions to the takeover partners.

As compared to the initial estimates reported in table 2.2, the FDIC estimates that by early 1983 falling interest rates had lowered the market value of the FDIC's loss in 1981–1982 failures of mutual savings banks by about one-third. However, with interest rates remaining highly volatile, even at their low point the full value of the FDIC's income-assistance agreements probably remained high enough to keep the true loss in the $2 billion range.

FDIC income-maintenance agreements have taken several forms. According to information in Brooks and Vartanian (1982, pp. 326–327), the time span of such assistance—unless terminated at the option of the bank or by the prospect of liquidation—runs between five and fifteen years. Contract provisions have comprised some or all of the following elements:

1. Income guarantees
a. FDIC payments to equal the difference between an annualized cost-of-funds index and the return on a designated base of supported assets.
b. FDIC payments to cover a portion of overhead costs.

2. Recapture provisions
a. A reduction in FDIC overhead payments should the cost-of-funds index decline below the return on the designated assets, with a return flow of income to the FDIC of 50 percent of the amount by which the positive interest margin exceeds overhead payments.
b. A payment to the FDIC of a portion of any positive interest spread.
c. A profit-or-loss sharing agreement whereby the FDIC receives a percentage of profits up to the amount of the FDIC's total assistance payments.

Additional FSLIC Innovations

As table 2.3 indicates, during the first five months of 1981 the failure of seven insured S&Ls cost the FSLIC about $344 million in estimated present value, 53 percent of which was paid in cash. This cash outflow ran about double the agency's cash inflow, forcing it to sell off at a discount over $150 million in long-term bonds, realizing substantial unbooked losses of its own in the process (Brooks and Vartanian 1982). Perhaps more significant the present value of FSLIC assistance in this case proved to be 22.4 percent of the assets of the institutions assisted. Had this same ratio of assistance to assets continued during the last twenty-three cases of 1981 and the forty-seven cases handled in 1982, FSLIC resources would have been fully pledged by mid-1982.

To conserve both its cash and its reported net worth, the FSLIC drastically altered its insolvency-resolution policies in May 1981, skew-

Table 2.3 FSLIC-assisted mergers during 1981 and the first quarter 1982 (in millions of dollars)

		Total cash outlays 1981					Estimated present value of total assistance, including contingent liabilities	
	Total assets	Contributions	Loans	Purchase of assets	Total outlay	% of assets	Total cost	% of assets
7 mergers, January 1–May 31, 1981[a]	$ 1,538	$180.8	$193.6	$557.7	$ 932.1	60.6%	$ 344	22.4%
23 cases, June 1–Dec. 31, 1981[b]	$12,335	$ 63.5	0	$ .2	$ 63.7	.5%	$ 633	5.1%
21 cases, January 1–March 31, 1982[c]	$12,168	$ 80.5	0	0	$ 80.5	.7%	$ 466	3.8%
Total cases	$26,041	$324.8	$193.6	$577.9	$1,076.3	4.1%	$1,443	5.5%

Source: H. Brent Beesley, "The FSLIC—Yesterday, Today, and Tomorrow," in Brooks and Vartanian (1982), pp. 33–63.
Note: All figures are subject to final adjustments per audits in process.
a. Home S&LA, Minneapolis; Security FS&LA, Statesville, N.C.; Franklin S&LA, Chicago; Guardian FS&LA, Northport, N.Y.; Arctic 1st Fed., Fairbanks, Alaska; Financial Security, Chicago; NY & Suburban FS&LA, New York.
b. Community FSLA, Washington, D.C.; First FSLA of New Bern, N.C.; First Financial, Bellaire, Tex.; County FS&LA, Rockville, Md.; First Fed. of Rochester; Franklin FS&LA, New York; Westside FS&LA, New York; Washington FS&LA, Miami Beach; Perpetual S&LA, Rapid City, S.D.; Lafayette FS&LA, St. Louis, Mo.; Hyde Park FS&LA, Chicago; Reserve S&LA, Chicago; First Fed. of Puerto Rico, Santurce, P.R.; Pan Am FS&LA, Santurce, P.R.; 1st FS&LA of Broward City, Ft. Lauderdale; Guaranty FS&LA, Baton Rouge, La.; Empire State FS&LA, White Plains, N.Y.; Palos S&LA, Chicago; Mohawk S&LA, Newark, N.J.; Boca Raton FS&LA, Boca Raton, Fla.; Security FS&LA, Sikeston, Md.; Hamiltonian FS&LA, La due, Mo.; Southern FS&LA, Pompano Beach, Fla.
c. First FS&LA, New Brunswick, N.J.; Inglewood FS&LA, Inglewood, Calif.; Buffalo S&LA, Houston; Civic S&LA, Irving, Texas; El Centro FS&LA, Dallas; Republic of Tex. SA, Houston; Royal FS&LA, Dallas; Hyde Park FS&LA, Chicago; Central Ill. BLA, Clinton, Ill.; Peach State FS&LA, Bremen, Ga.; First of Sylvania, Ga.; Guaranty FS&LA, Adel, Ga.; United FS&LA, Smyrna, Ga.; Morgan Park, Chicago; Talman Home FS&LA, Chicago; Unity SA, Schamburg, Ill.; North West FS&LA, Chicago; Alliance S&LA, Chicago; Ninth FS&LA, New York; Knickerbocker FS&LA, New York; Hartford FS&LA, Hartford, Conn.

ing subsequent merger assistance payments toward noncash and contingent payments such as income-maintenance agreements and particularly toward implicit forms of value. FSLIC allowances for possible future losses under contribution agreements were $1,008 million in 1983 and $705 million in 1982. The major sources of implicit or undisclosed values have been indemnifications against postmerger claims (such as against unfunded pension liabilities) and regulatory exemptions granted to takeover institutions: the right to enter out-of-state markets (which by the end of 1982 had been conferred in roughly twenty cases) and the right to use purchase accounting principles that let an acquirer book the value of otherwise unbookable assets in ways that temporarily improve its reported future cash flow and conventional (nonaugmented) balance sheet.

In addition the FSLIC evolved a form of joint conservatorship known as the phoenix plan. This plan was applied in seven cases where failing institutions in a single region could be combined into a single corporation (the phoenix institution rising from the ashes of the multiple failure) and made viable by injections of FSLIC cash or notes. As compared to deposit payoff, the phoenix approach has several advantages for the FSLIC insurance fund. First, it can eliminate some management expense and effect combinations that might otherwise be prohibited by antitrust laws. The cost of any antitrust exemptions is shifted to competing deposit institutions and to deposit institution customers in the phoenix's market area. Second, by retaining the option to merge the phoenix or any of its components when and as a cost-effective alternative develops, the FSLIC preserves low-cost deposit certificates on the books of the institution while establishing the agency's right to claim the price appreciation that these short-funded institutions may expect to experience in the event of an interest rate decline.

The Slide toward De Facto Nationalization

Net worth certificates, income-maintenance agreements, phoenix institutions, and the package of ownership claims negotiated in the Continental Illinois rescue represent documentable back-door devices by which the federal government's equity stake in deposit institutions increased substantially during the early 1980s. Because phoenix institutions combine operational control with federal ownership, they best exemplify the slide toward de facto nationalization of troubled institutions that mispriced federal deposit insurance entails. In effect phoenix institutions are nationalized institutions in which the FSLIC exercises a degree of control that is equivalent to voting government-owned stock. Beginning in December 1982 after thrift institution balance sheets improved with the decline of interest rates observed during the last half of 1982, the FSLIC formally moved to solicit takeover bids to return phoenix institutions to the private sector. With only a few institutions to sell, transferring phoenix firms back to private ownership this time around raises no insuperable problems. However, if interest rates remain highly volatile and deposit insurance premiums remain insensitive to client risk exposure, the FDIC and FSLIC may acquire more institutions in the next crunch than they can sell off smoothly at nondistress prices.

References

Aharoni, Yair. 1981. *The No-Risk Society*. Chatham, N.J.: Chatham House Publishers.

Barnett, Robert E.; Horvitz, Paul M.; and Silverberg, Stanley C. 1977. "Deposit Insurance: The Present System and Some Alternatives." *Banking Law Journal* 94 (April): 304–332.

Black, Fisher; Miller, Merton; and Posner, Richard. 1978. "An Approach to the Regulation of Bank Holding Companies." *Journal of Business* 51 (July): 379–411.

Brooks, Thomas A., and Vartanian, Thomas P. 1982. *Thrifts Acquisitions and Supervisory Problems: The F.D.I.C. and F.H.L.B.B. Speak*. New York: Law & Business/Harcourt Brace Jovanovich.

McCulloch, J. Huston. 1983. "Interest-Risk Sensitive Deposit Insurance Premia: Adaptive Conditional Heteroscedastic Estimates." Unpublished manuscript. Ohio State University, June.

Marcus, Alan J., and Shaked, Israel. 1982. "The Valuation of FDIC Deposit Insurance: Empirical Estimates Using the Options Pricing Framework." Boston University School of Management, July.

Marvell, Thomas B. 1969. *The Federal Home Loan Bank Board*. New York: Praeger.

Merton, Robert C. 1977. "An Analytic Derivation of the Cost of Deposit Insurance and Loan Guarantees: An Application of Modern Option Pricing Theory." *Journal of Banking and Finance* 1 (June): 3–11.

Miller, Randall J. 1981. "Are Deposit Insurance Assessments Too High?" *Bankers Magazine* 164 (March–April): 44–46.

Silverberg, Stanley, and Flechsig, Theodore G. 1978. "The Case for 100% Insurance of Demand Deposits." *Issues in Bank Regulation* (Winter): 38–44.

Chapter 3

Structural Weaknesses in the U.S. Deposit Insurance System

Praised for nearly fifty years as a fabulously successful innovation in banking regulation, federal deposit insurance is showing signs of old age. Like a house built 50 years ago in a geologically active neighborhood, its foundations have developed some noticeable cracks.

Deposit insurance straddles two acknowledged fault lines. Both emanate from the danger than an insurer itself may become insolvent. The first concerns the imperfect diversifiability of deposit insurance risk. Diversification difficulties help to explain the decision to lodge the insurance function in government agencies rather than in profit-oriented private firms. Important types of losses on individual deposit insurance contracts are not stochastically independent. Table 3.1 shows that the number of problem banks (those that the FDIC judges to be in financial difficulty) moves up and down with the level of economic activity. Over the business cycle it tends to follow the rate of business failures with a lag, peaking a good while after macroeconomic activity reaches a cyclical low. Because macroeconomic fluctuations affect all banks at approximately the same time, a potential for a ruinous bunching of insurance claims exists. Of course, so extreme a bunching is an event that, as the nation's chief agency for economic stabilization and its lender of last resort, the Federal Reserve is charged with preventing. Nevertheless the possibility of a massive chain of failures prevents private providers of deposit insurance from issuing a guarantee that is inherently as perfect (at least in nominal terms) as one that is backed up explicitly or implicitly by the money-creating power of a sovereign government. It is possible that a government insurer may become insolvent, but the probability of its defaulting on depositor claims is lessened by political pressures that potential losers can exert on incumbent politicians, who have a strong self-interest in fulfilling government commitments to the electorate. To allow deposit insurance agencies to renege on so serious a set of promises would alienate a large number of voters. Responding to such pressure during the election year of 1982 Congress passed a joint resolution putting the full faith and credit of the U.S. Treasury behind the guarantees of the deposit insurance agencies.

For creditors of insured institutions government operation increases the probability of an ex post government bailout of the insurance fund in the event of a systemwide financial crisis. In raising the funds to finance a bailout operation, the government would necessarily spread the costs onto other parties in the economy. The precise distribution of the burden of adjustment would vary depending on whether the government chose to resort to debt financing, reduced spending, increased federal tax rates, or an inflationary surge in governmental money creation.

At the same time assigning the insurance function to a government agency sacrifices everyday cost efficiency. Bureaucratic incentives make agency personnel more responsive in the short run to political than to economic pressure. Political pressure focuses on the hardships that individual failures threaten to impose on particular members of society and on the danger that a failure might initiate a sequence of systemwide collapse. It focuses on events whose impact on policy goals is in some way rooted in previous experience. The banking collapse of the 1930s burns in public memory with sufficient intensity that no contemporary bureaucrat is willing to risk bringing on another, especially when the costs of bailout operations may be readily shifted out of agency budgets onto surviving institutions and taxpayers at large. In contrast to political pressure economic pressure flows from changes in opportunities for anticipated profit and loss. Though real, such opportunities initially are hypothetical rather than experiential. Red tape and a desire to minimize negative political feedback in the short run encourage bureaucrats to respond in lagged fashion to microeconomic changes in the insurance environment.

The second fault line emanates from the informational disadvantages and adverse selection to which every insurer is exposed. The principal reason that a deposit institution maintains a capital account is to make credible its capacity to absorb the risks inherent in its operations. Given

Table 3.1 Number of problem banks listed by FDIC compared with number of business failures and business failure rate, 1968–1981

Year	Number of problem banks	Number of business failures (thousands)	Business failure rate per 10,000 listed concerns
1968	240	9.6	39
1969	216	9.2	37
1970	251	10.7	44
1971	239	10.3	42
1972	190	9.6	38
1973	155	9.3	36
1974	181	9.9	38
1975	347	11.4	43
1976	385	9.6	35
1977	368	7.9	28
1978	342	6.6	24
1979	287	7.6	28
1980	217	11.7	42
1981	223	17.0	61
Mid-1982	277 (on Sept. 29)	12.3 (through first week in July)	n.a.
Late-1982	320 (on Oct. 19)	19.7 (through Oct. 14)	n.a.
1982	369	24.9	88
Mid-1983	450–475 (on Sept. 15)	31.0[a] (annualized first half)	n.a.
1983	642	31.3	110
Early 1984	667 (on March 31)	100.1	n.a.
Mid-1984	715 (on June 30)	87.0	n.a.
1984	847	88.3	n.a.

Sources: For problem banks: 1968–1976, compiled by Joseph Sinkey from fourth-quarter problem bank lists prepared by FDIC Division of Bank Supervision. 1977–1983: Year-end figures cited in FDIC *Annual Reports.* Intrayear figures: September 29, 1983, correspondence from Robert P. Gough, associate director, Division of Bank Supervision, FDIC; later figures are based on reports in the *American Banker* of talks given by William Isaac and telephone calls to other FDIC staff members. For business failures: *Data Resources U.S. Review,* June 1982 (prepared originally by Dun & Bradstreet) and subsequent telephone calls to Dun & Bradstreet offices.
Notes: FDIC procedures for classifying problem banks were revised in 1980. Because in 1984 Dun & Bradstreet converted its reports to an index number basis, 1984 figures are reported as a percentage of the base period, October 1983. The major point is that, although the rate of business failure peaked in 1983, the problem bank list continued to grow throughout 1984.
   a. Preliminary estimate.

insurance coverage and a schedule of premiums, deposit insurers must anticipate that their clients will desire less capital and undertake an adverse selection of portfolio risks. Signing an insurance contract alters the benefits and costs of voluntarily taking additional risk (Mayers and Smith 1982). This inevitable change in incentives exposes every insurer to what is called moral hazard: the risk that insurance coverage leads insured parties deliberately to pursue risks that in an uninsured state they would not take. For deposit insurers moral hazard is especially difficult because deposit institution managers are better informed than agency personnel about the economic consequences of the risks they take. As figure 1.1 should make clear, many forms of voluntary risk-taking by deposit institutions are simultaneously easy for an insured's management to conceal and hard for an insurer to diversify against. When a large portion of an institution's portfolio risk can be shifted onto an unwary insurer at the margin, riskier assets and additional leverage become attractive to its portfolio managers.

Damage wrought by either one of these two structural faults tends to introduce reinforcing behavior on the other front. In particular whenever operative techniques and categories of deposit institution risk-taking expand rapidly, lags associated with government operation leave U.S. deposit insurance agencies doubly vulnerable to adverse selection.

By early 1982 public confidence in the ability of U.S. deposit insurance agencies to surmount the risk bunching and moral hazard problems had declined noticeably. In part this was because relevant categories of deposit institution risk-taking had expanded rapidly during the 1970s. The risks a deposit institution incurs flow from its dual role as an institutional investor and as a producer of financial services. Figure 1.1 depicts these risks schematically.

Four forms of risk have grown dramatically in importance during the last decade and a half: affiliated institution risk, interest volatility risk, technological risk, and regulatory risk. During the same interval making loans to governments and government-sponsored firms in less-developed and Eastern European countries exploited a category of credit risk (country risk) that, presumably because of a political conflict with the nation's grander foreign policy goals, was too long left unregulated. To a considerable degree growth in these risks was stimulated by regulatory lags inherent in controlling deposit insurance subsidies to unregulated forms of risk. For example, not until September 1983 did the Office of the Comptroller of the Currency form a special watchdog unit on country risk. Several varieties of previously unregulated risks are now beginning to be regulated systematically. In particular the International Lending Act of 1983 (which accompanied November 1983 legislation to expand resources of the International Monetary Fund) requires federal deposit institution regulators to develop extensive reporting requirements and to impose special capital reserves on U.S. banks that make foreign loans.

Affiliated institution risk comes in two varieties: double leveraging of deposit institution capital (which means financing increases in an institution's pool of equity funds by issuing debt against a second-tier corporation—a "holding company"—that owns the corresponding stock) and affiliated institutions' implicit entitlement to draw on the financial resources of a related deposit institution in case of trouble. Since the mid-1960s, expansion in commercial bank use of the holding company form of organization has developed in response to favorable regulatory and tax treatment afforded nonbank subsidiaries of these companies (Eisenbeis 1983). Double leveraging was encouraged because, at the same time that federal authorities pressured banks to maintain higher-than-desired capital ratios, they allowed banks to substitute debt finance by a parent holding company for true capital, thereby increasing the effective level of leverage applicable on a consolidated basis. Although double leveraging was closely monitored by federal banking agencies, corrective regulatory action was slow in coming, especially for large banks. Because nonbank subsidiaries were more lightly regulated than the banking component of the organization, it was profitable to spin off more and more operations from the banking component to nonbank affiliates and to coordinate the consolidated product line at the parent level. Moreover, through time, the set of financial activities that the Federal Reserve Board permits affiliated nonbank institutions to undertake has expanded sharply. Until the late 1970s Federal Reserve policies presumed that it was possible to isolate the financial condition and activities of a banking subsidiary from that of its holding company affiliates. The lack of success these policies encountered suggests that regulatory isolation of a subset of affiliated enterprises is not a realistic objective. Affiliated institutions' implicit claim on the resources of related deposit institutions is vividly illustrated by two cases. First and more recently, antidilution covenants attached to debt issued by the holding company of Continental Illinois National Bank prevented the FDIC from taking an explicit equity position in the bank without simultaneously bailing out the creditors of the holding company. Such covenants make a mockery of the policy of encouraging bank managers to shift leverage from the balance sheets of banks to those of their parent holding companies. Second, the energy that banks put into keeping allied real estate investment trusts afloat in the face of obvious market value insolvencies brought on by the 1974–1975 recession shows their concern for protecting corporations whose names and activities are intertwined with those of the bank.

Federal regulators were also slow to respond to client adverse selection with respect to three other types of risk: financial technology risk, interest volatility risk, and country risk. In the face of the deposit insurance subsidy to unregulated risk, this lack of response encouraged deposit institutions to make riskier business-organization, financing, and loan decisions than they would have otherwise. First, ceilings on explicit deposit rates led deposit institution managers to search for ways of paying household customers implicit interest. (Implicit interest is paid whenever an institution performs services for accountholders at fees that lie below the institution's marginal cost of providing these services.) Gearing up to offer these services often required large commitments of capital and a substantial exposure to risks of obsolescence. With properly priced deposit insurance, deposit institutions would have been less eager to expand their retail-oriented branch office networks just when developments in communications and computer technology were beginning to make off-premises automated teller machines and in-home and in-office banking connections realistic substitutes for traditional branch offices. In this and other respects regulatory distortions complicate the adoption of new technologies for producing financial services. Second, in the face of changes in Federal Reserve policy procedures that dramatically increased the volatility of interest rate fluctuations, most thrift institutions and some commercial banks maintained (and some of them even increased) imbalances between the average futurity of their assets and liabilities. Congressional interest in promoting home-ownership made it hard for the FDIC and FSLIC to act to penalize institutions that took interest volatility risk in the form of financing long-term mortgage lending with short-term liabilities. Third, commercial banks encouraged private and government borrowers in foreign countries to weigh themselves down with debts whose periodic interest burden, without a continuation of secularly accelerating U.S. inflation, was bound to exceed their anticipated ability to earn sufficient foreign exchange to service the debt. Congressional interest in winning a cold war competition for the political support of less-developed and Eastern bloc countries made it hard for federal examiners to offer forceful criticisms of these loans.

Current understanding of the riskiness of these decisions benefits from hindsight. In the 1970s few deposit institution managers professed to appreciate how risky contemporary strategies for market expansion might prove ex post. But mainstream financial analysts were warning them of danger. In calculations made in 1978 with data covering the years 1946 through 1977, McCulloch (1981) shows that the value of deposit insurance guarantees increases dramatically as an institution's net worth declines and (for a given liability structure) as the maturity of asset holdings increases.

For our purposes what matters is the proposition that, on average, deposit institution managers had a better (even if imperfect) appreciation of applicable portfolio risks than government deposit insurers did. Incentives established in deposit insurance contracts made additional portfolio risk attractive to deposit institution managers, while government ownership slowed the reaction time and constrained the responses of deposit insurance personnel. If deposit insurance had been lodged in the private sector, the absence of political restraints and concern for insurer and job survival would have made insurance executives and examiners in the field quicker to perceive the extent of the risks that deposit institution portfolio activities were shifting onto the deposit insurance funds.

Repayment problems for borrowers translate into collection problems for lenders. In the same way, deteriorating deposit institution balance sheets spell trouble for U.S. deposit insurance agencies. Backed up by the Fed and by the general taxpayer, federal insurance agencies are the financial system's risk-takers of second-last resort. This makes them contingent suppliers for their clients not just of liquidity but of equity capital. When ruinous losses causing market value insolvencies are experienced by deposit institutions, deposit insurers have the job of supplying whatever amount of equity funds is necessary to prevent insured depositors from being at risk.

To quantify the stakes, every insurance agency guarantee of an institution's deposit debt may be thought of as a book entry security whose discounted present value belongs on the balance sheets of insured and insurer alike. The actuarial value of each particular guarantee rises when the insured's economic prospects decline and falls when these prospects improve. Although the prospects of individual banks are only imperfectly correlated, the aggregate value of individual guarantees is subject to risk bunching. Beginning in 1982 unexpectedly high and volatile interest rates combined with prolonged recession to push the number of problem banks and the aggregate value of deposit insurance guarantees to record heights. Although the value of these guarantees declined with a temporary fall in interest rates after mid-1982, it surged again in 1984.

Deposit Insurance Goals and the Structure of Premiums

Deposit insurance has two ostensible goals: to prevent widespread deposit institution failures and to protect the consolidated interests of small individual depositors. Responsibility for both goals is shared with other regulators (particularly with the Federal Reserve System, whose span of regulatory control extends to the entire financial sector). The FDIC and FSLIC pursue the goals set for the insurance system in two ways. First, they guarantee the deposit debt of every insured deposit institution up to a fixed amount per depositor. Over time Congress has increased this amount from $2,500 to $100,000. Second, with the assistance of companion state and federal regulatory authorities, they restrict competitive activity and seek to penalize overaggressive risk-taking by insured institutions. Restrictions on competitive activity restrain an institution's capacity for expansion in the geographical area spanned by its office locations, expansion by merger or entry into related and unrelated lines of business, and expansion through price competition for deposits. Most of these restrictions are intended to limit the possibility that competitive activity by one deposit institution will undermine the solvency of another. Activity to limit client risk-taking aims at controlling risks of insolvency by imposing capital requirements and other restrictions on bank activities and by regularly monitoring the safety and soundness of client operations.

The structure of explicit FDIC premiums is designed to meet agency operating costs, to cover disbursements occasioned by closing or assisting the merger of failing institutions, and to maintain a modest insurance fund. Each year, insured banks are assessed in semiannual installments a rebatable 1/12 of 1 percent of their assessable deposits. From 1962 through 1980 annual rebates were mandated by law at two-thirds of assessments collected, net of deductions for FDIC expenses and provisions for losses. Starting July 1, 1981, the mandated rebate level was reduced to 60 percent, with lesser or larger amounts allowed whenever accumulated reserves exceed or fall short of stipulated limits. During the 1970s the net explicit charge for FDIC insurance averaged less than 1/25 of 1 percent of assessable deposits. Due to a sharp increase in losses sustained by the FDIC in 1980 and 1981, the net explicit insurance premium doubled in 1981, to 1/14 of 1 percent. The net charge has stayed in this vicinity ever since, rising to 1/13 of 1 percent in 1982 and falling back to 1/14 of 1 percent in 1983. The multibillion dollar cost of rescuing Continental Illinois may drive the net explicit premium to record highs in 1984 and beyond. This jump in net explicit charges is spreading the cost of rescuing the depositors of failing firms across the universe of surviving competitors, irrespective of how conservatively an individual institution might have managed its own portfolio. Because almost all states require even state-chartered banks to carry deposit insurance, low-risk institutions are effectively forced to assist the government to underwrite the risks that their high-flying competitors take.

FSLIC explicit premiums are fixed at 1/12 of 1 percent of assessable deposits. Amounts in excess of deductions for designated agency expenses and provisions for current losses are not subject to rebate, but

Table 3.2 Average number and average aggregate deposits of U.S. banks closed per year because of financial difficulties, for various subperiods, 1934–1982

Years	Average number of closings per year			Average deposits in banks closed (millions)			
	All banks	Non-insured banks	Insured banks	All banks	Insured banks only		
					Total	Without disbursements by FDIC	With disbursements by FDIC
1934–1940	64.2	13.1	51.1	$68.2	$62.3	$0.1	$62.3
1941–1950	7.3	1.2	6.1	10.3	9.9	0.1	9.8
1951–1960	4.3	1.5	2.8	11.5	10.5	3.7	6.8
1961–1970	6.3	1.3	5.0	34.2	33.5	0.3	33.2
1971–1980	8.3	0.4	7.9	537.2	529.1		529.1
1971–1974	4.8	0.5	4.3	694.8	675.0		675.0
1975–1981	10.6	0.3	10.3	916.9	916.7		916.7
				Total deposits in insured banks closed (millions)			
1981	10		10	3,826.0	3,826.0		3,826.0
1982	42		42	9,908.4	9,908.4		9,908.4
1983	48		48	5,441.6	5,441.6		5,441.6
1984 (through July 12)	44	n.a.	44	n.a.	1,680.8	n.a.	1,680.8
1984	79	n.a.	79	n.a.	2,932.0	n.a.	2,932.0

Source: Averages calculated from FDIC, *1981 Annual Report*, vol. 1. Other data from *1982 Annual Report* and *1983 Annual Report* and from a list of 1984 bank failures prepared by FDIC staff, in which assets rather than deposits were given for one savings bank.

Table 3.3 Ten largest U.S. commercial bank failures in FDIC history

Bank	Year failure resolved	Total deposits at resolution date (millions)	Deposits adjusted for interim inflation (millions)
Continental Illinois Bank and Trust Co., Chicago	1984	$30,000 (approx.)[a]	$30,000
Franklin National Bank, New York	1974	1,445	2,769
United States National Bank, San Diego	1973	932	1,943
Banco Credit y Ahorro Ponceno, Ponce, Puerto Rico	1978	608	892
United American Bank, Knoxville, Tennessee	1983	585	599
First National Bank of Midland, Midland, Texas	1983	574	587
Penn Square Bank, Oklahoma City	1982	470	501
Hamilton National Bank of Chattanooga, Chattanooga, Tennessee	1976	336	560
Abilene National Bank, Abilene, Texas	1982	310	331
American City Bank, Los Angeles	1983	255	261

Source: FDIC *Annual Reports* and discussions with FDIC personnel about the rescue of Continental Illinois.

Notes: The largest pre-FDIC failure was the over $200 million Bank of United States in 1930. This failure would be the fourth largest on an inflation-adjusted basis. The inflation adjustment uses the implicit price deflator for GNP and the flash estimate for May 1984, as published in *Business Cycle Developments* (June 1984 and August 1983 issues).

a. The Continental Illinois banking corporation did not fail. Rather, most of its stock was effectively nationalized. Also the institution's size would be recorded as 50 percent larger if we included nondeposit borrowing (for example, federal funds purchases, repurchase agreements, and borrowing from the Fed and FDIC).

Table 3.4 FSLIC insolvency resolution in recent years

	1969	1970	1971	1972	1973	1974
FSLIC acquisitions and realizations of problem case assets and investment securities, 1971-1981 (millions of dollars)						
Net acquisitions of investment securities	n.a.	n.a.	187.1[a]	182.6[a]	354.6[a]	343.4
Acquisitions of problem-case assets	n.a.	n.a.	4.8	5.1	1.7	12.9
Contributions to insured institutions	n.a.	n.a.	1.0	3.3[b]	3.7[b]	6.1
Realizations on sales of assets acquired from insured institutions	n.a.	n.a.	65.6	31.2	33.1	10.9
S&L mergers, insurance settlement actions, and year-end FSLIC and S&L reserve ratios, 1969-1980						
Mergers of insured S&Ls	83	118	132	107	124	132
Supervisory mergers	n.a.	n.a.	n.a.	n.a.	n.a.	n.a.
Insurance settlement actions	0	0	1	4	5	2
Book value of FSLIC reserves (billions of dollars)	2.8	2.9	3.0	3.1	3.5	3.8
FSLIC reserves as a percent of all accounts of insured members of insured institutions	2.14	2.05	1.77	1.56	1.56	1.60
Ratio of net worth accounts to total assets on the books of insured S&Ls (percent)	6.92	6.75	6.34	6.01	6.23	6.20
FHLB advances as a percent of total assets of insured S&Ls	5.7	6.1	3.9	3.3	5.6	7.4

Sources: FSLIC Annual Reports (April issues of the *Federal Home Loan Bank Board Journal* from 1970 through 1983), *Savings and Loan Sourcebook* (1981 and 1982) and *Savings and Home Financing Source Book* (1979), Federal Home Loan Bank Board, *Combined Financial Statements* (1984), U.S. Government Accounting Office, Examination of FHLBB and FSLIC financial statements for years ended December 31, 1983, and 1982 (1984), and Gould (1984).

a. Net change in market value of government securities portfolio in 1971, 1972, and 1973.

b. Net change in "allowance for estimated losses—contribution agreements" in 1971, 1972, and 1973.

c. Thirty individual cases were resolved in these twenty-three mergers, involving an estimated present value of $977 million in assistance and contingent liabilities and four interstate acquisitions.

1975	1976	1977	1978	1979	1980	1981	1982	1983
361.9	418.1	388.2	413.8	494.1	−635.5	−289.9	0.0	420.7
59.9	13.3	13.8	27.6	4.8	1,215.5	543.5	383.2	
12.4	15.5	21.8	21.5	24.8	41.6	318.0	596.7[d]	895.2
37.4	51.7	6.9	10.1	8.7	39.6	125.5	95.8	
111	85	44	44	37	141	296	425	122[f]
n.a.	n.a.	n.a.	n.a.	n.a.	21	56	167	27[f]
2	6	3	2	3	11	23[c]	47[d]	21[f]
4.1	4.5	4.9	5.3	5.8	6.5	6.2	6.3	6.4
1.48	1.37	1.29	1.26	1.27	1.29	1.11	1.14	0.96
5.81	5.58	5.45	5.51	5.58	5.26	4.23	3.69[e]	4.02[e]
5.3	4.1	4.4	6.2	7.1	7.6	9.6	9.3[e]	7.0[e]

d. In 1982 a slight discrepancy exists between the *Annual Report* and other sources. The *Report* shows $503.9 million in contributions. The figure given is taken from the 1984 GAO audit report on the FSLIC. The *Report* indicates forty-seven FSLIC-assisted mergers involving over seventy-five disappearing associations. Gould (1984) reports forty-three assisted mergers involving sixty-five associations. Total cash outlay in these cases was $201.6 million. The estimated present calue of 1982 assistance and contingent liabilities in $1,131.2 million, of which only $201.6 million represents cash payments.

e. Reported on a new accounting basis that was adopted following a July 1982 regulatory reclassification of a particular set of liabilities as deductions from asset accounts.

f. Updated figures by Gould (1984) of her published figures to take them through the year.

to replenish reserves the FHLB can (as in 1985) levy an additional premium of up to 1/8 of 1 percent.

Agency Loss Experience and Risk Exposure

Elements of FDIC and FSLIC loss experience and loss exposure are summarized in tables 3.2 through 3.5. Unfortunately the two agencies do not report parallel information. Table 3.2 shows that the average size of banks closed and, more important, the average annual losses the FDIC has had to cover jumped in the 1970s and continued to rise into the 1980s. As table 3.3 indicates, the ten largest commercial bank failures in FDIC history have occurred since 1973, with the bulk since 1981. Assisting the mergers of the fourteen large mutual savings banks cited in table 2.2 helped make FDIC disbursements particularly heavy after 1981.

Table 3.4 shows that FSLIC and S&L industry balance sheet ratios deteriorated over the 1970s. In 1980 and 1981 the FSLIC began to experience increased claims from settling the affairs of failing institutions. Spurts in FSLIC purchases of assets from troubled institutions and so-called contributions of FSLIC funds to assist supervisory mergers and deposit assumptions forced a substantial sell-off of investment assets in 1980 and 1981. Beginning in late 1981 FSLIC contributions to a supervisory merger or acquisition have taken the form of contingent liabilities that guarantee a minimum level of performance on assets that are transferred from a failing institution.

Table 3.5 documents a burst in U.S. bank involvement in foreign lending and depositing over the last decade, especially in 1980 and 1981. Some of these outflows represent credits to Soviet bloc countries. These and all other loans to foreign governmental entities are fundamentally different from private loans. Instead of being backed by physical assets employed in a productive enterprise, they are backed by the (economically limited) faith and credit of a foreign government. If a country's rulers choose not to meet contractual payments, a borrower has fewer legal remedies than are available for use against a recalcitrant domestic borrower. Because lawsuits brought against a sovereign government are not likely to fare well in that country's courts, banks that

Table 3.5 Annual dollar increase in foreign claims of U.S. banks, 1971–1983

Year	Net Change in Claims (billions of dollars)		
	Short term	Long term	Total
1971	2.4	0.6	3.0
1972	2.2	1.3	3.5
1973	5.0	0.9	6.0
1974	18.3	1.2	19.5
1975	11.2	2.4	13.5
1976	19.0	2.4	21.4
1977	10.7	0.8	11.4
1978	n.a.	n.a.	33.7
1979	n.a.	n.a.	26.2
1980	n.a.	n.a.	46.8
1981	n.a.	n.a.	84.2
1982	n.a.	n.a.	111.1
1983	n.a.	n.a.	25.4

Sources: 1971–1980: *Survey of Current Business* (June issues). 1981–1983: telephone conversation with Russ Scholl, Commerce Department.
Notes: From 1978 on, the *Survey of Current Business* no longer differentiates short-term and long-term claims. Detail may not add to total because of rounding. These claims include foreign loans to nonbanks, interbank deposits at foreign banks, and claims on foreign banking affiliates. On March 31, 1983, $419.8 billion in foreign loans was reported as outstanding.

lend to sovereign governments are subject to political as well as economic risks. Potential variation in the economic ability and political willingness of a government to make timely payments of interest and principal on its or its citizens' foreign debts is called sovereign risk.

Table 3.6 reports the net external position of selected countries to external banks in seventeen major countries between 1982 and 1984. Although it is impossible to prove that any particular set of deposits supports any particular class of loans, many U.S. banks advertised their expansion of foreign loans as petrodollars that they had "recycled" to government entities in non-OPEC developing countries. When first extended, these multibillion dollar loans to Communist and Third World countries were declared a proud achievement of modern capitalism, one that manifested the flexibility and efficiency of the international banking system. When the riskiness of these loans was questioned, spokespersons for the banking community proclaimed these loans to

Table 3.6 Comparison of 1982 and 1984 net external positions of banks in selected countries, ranked by size of net debt in first quarter of 1982 (billions of U.S. dollars)

Country	Net balance of foreign-held assets and liabilities	
	March 1982	March 1984
Mexico	46.3	47.3
Brazil	46.2	54.9
Japan	43.7	45.1
Germany, Federal Republic of	31.3	32.0
Belgium-Luxembourg	20.9	14.1
Italy	20.8	21.8
Argentina	16.4	18.3
France	16.1	26.6
Venezuela	15.2	16.2
Poland	13.3	9.6
South Korea	13.2	15.9
Sweden	11.9	14.1
Panama	11.2	8.3
Canada	10.5	7.4
South Africa	10.0	14.8
Denmark	9.9	12.1
Portugal	8.7	7.4
Soviet Union	7.9	4.5
Germany, Democratic Republic of	7.7	4.7
Yugoslavia	7.4	7.5
Australia	7.0	13.2
Hong Kong	6.6	4.7
Chile	6.3	8.1
Hungary	6.0	5.7
Spain	5.4	6.8

Source: Bank for International Settlements, "International banking developments—first quarter 1984," Basle, Switzerland, table 5.
Note: Net external position is calculated as debt held by external banks (those in Austria, Belgium-Luxembourg, Denmark, Finland [1984 only], France, West Germany, Ireland, Italy, Netherlands, Norway [1984 only], Spain [1984 only], Sweden, Switzerland, United Kingdom, Canada, Japan, and the United States) net of liabilities of these banks to the designated country.

be fundamentally less risky than they might appear. They counted on political competition between the East and the West to guarantee implicitly that, in the event that borrowing countries could not meet contractual obligations from their own resources, the USSR, the United States, or multilateral agencies (such as the International Monetary Fund or World Bank) would step up to bail them out. However, between 1982 and 1984, although these implicit guarantors have helped, they have proved surprisingly reluctant to assist borrower nations to surmount cash flow burden generated by unexpectedly high real interest rates. To avert explicit defaults in contractual flows of interest and principal, well-publicized financial difficulties experienced by several of the largest borrower nations (Brazil, Argentina, Mexico, and Poland) have so far been papered over by a series of accounting tricks: interest deferrals, loan restructurings, and semilenient interventions by the International Monetary Fund. Accounted at market value, these involuntary concessions to borrower nations amount to substantial implicit write-downs of affected loan contracts below their book values.

These sudden alterations in the size of failing institutions and in the role of foreign debt mark an important change in the character of FDIC and FSLIC risk exposure. During this same era the International Banking Act of 1978 further expanded the riskiness of FDIC operations by adding U.S. branches of foreign banks to the list of institutions eligible for FDIC insurance.

At both the FDIC and FSLIC, insurance liabilities are supported by assessment income, a fund of earning assets, ability to draw on an emergency backup line of credit at the U.S. Treasury, and the right to levy emergency supplemental assessments on client institutions. During the 1970s statutory authority to borrow from the Treasury remained constant at $3.0 billion for the FDIC and $0.75 billion for the FSLIC, even though deposits at insured institutions rose much faster than either client net worth or deposit insurance reserves. Although Congress passed a joint resolution in March 1982 that put the full faith and credit of the federal government behind insurance agency guarantees, it failed to establish an explicit mechanism by which the agencies could draw on Treasury resources if they ran short of funds. This leads one to conjecture that, in a crisis, the resolution could serve to justify a merger of the two agencies or large loans or grants from the Federal Reserve to either the FDIC or the FSLIC.

For the FDIC the ratio of reserves to insured deposits fell from 1.50 percent on December 31, 1963, to a low of 1.16 percent on December 31, 1980. With the rapid growth of large denomination deposits and managed liabilities in nondeposit forms, the ratio of the insurance fund to the total noncash assets of insured institutions stood far lower, at 0.70 percent. During the same interval, net worth and surplus accounts at insured institutions declined relative to deposit and noncash assets as well.

By increasing coverage per depositor from $40,000 to $100,000 the Depository Institutions Deregulation and Monetary Control Act of 1980 contributed to the declining trend by expanding the ratio of insured to total deposits. But it also reduced the rebate level and required the FDIC to reestablish a higher coverage ratio for its insurance reserves. Despite unfavorable loss experience betweeen 1981 and 1983, by year-end 1983 the FDIC had raised its reserve ratio to 1.22 percent. But this ratio takes no account of the implicit guarantees the FDIC may be said to extend to uninsured deposit and nondeposit debt through its oft-stated preference for resolving deposit institution failures by offering capital assistance or arranging an assisted merger or deposit assumption rather than liquidating a failed bank (Barnett, Horvitz, and Silverberg 1977). During the 1980s declines in bank capital and increases in uninsured categories of bank and bank holding company debt greatly increased the effective value of contingent claims against FDIC reserves; hence, the recorded increase in FDIC reserve coverage is not impressive.

FSLIC reserves are reported as a percentage of all accounts of insured members of all insured institutions. This ratio more than doubled between 1963 and 1969, rising from 1.01 to 2.14 percent. But by 1981 the ratio had fallen back to 1.23 percent. Table 3.4 tracks this decline and shows a concomitant fall in the book value of the ratio of net worth to assets on the books of insured S&Ls. In turn, estimates of unrealized capital losses associated with S&Ls' short-funded holdings of mortgages indicate that the market value of S&L net worth accounts is almost certainly negative (Kane 1982). Since 1978 advances from the Home Loan Bank System have exceeded even the overstated book value of

S&L net worth accounts. By 1981 advances ran more than twice the value of S&Ls' recorded equity resources.

Deteriorating Public Confidence

Since early 1982 managers of federal deposit insurance agencies have found it increasingly difficult to maintain public confidence in banks and thrift institutions. The erosion in confidence that first made itself felt in 1982 responded to both an accelerating rate of decline of net worth coverage at thrift institutions and declining reserve coverage at the insurance agencies. The severity of public doubts may be measured in part by the rising interest cost paid on uninsured borrowing by insured institutions. It also shows up in decreases in the threshold ratio of net worth to assets at client institutions that regulators use to define a problem institution. In effect widespread insufficiencies of capital at client institutions led bureaucrats perversely to recalibrate their standards for capital adequacy to reduce the implied caseload to a magnitude that their supervisory staff could handle. In effect the equity stake of deposit insurers outgrew their managerial resources.

Table 3.7 documents cyclical movements in the risk premium that market participants attach to the uninsured portion of ninety-day certificates of deposit (CDs) at commercial banks. Undoubtedly observed premiums would be even larger if it were not for investors' perceptions of the FDIC's propensity to resolve large-bank failures in ways that keep uninsured depositors whole. At any date the risk premium may be interpreted as a market-determined insurance charge that uninsured lenders impose on a deposit institution for issuing formally uninsured liabilities of ninety-day maturity. That these premiums always exceed the common FDIC and FSLIC premium of 1/12 of 1 percent is particularly telling. Because these risk premiums rise and fall cyclically with the level of interest rates, allowances for the declining market value of the net worth of short-funded institutions and for bearing interest-volatility risk may constitute the dominant components of these returns. Confirming the hypothesis that recognition of problem situations by regulators lags that of the market, data displayed in table 3.1 on the number of FDIC-supervised problem banks tend to lag not only

Table 3.7 Risk premium on large-denomination certificates of deposit, issued by large commercial banks, 1964–1984 (percentage per annum)

Date	Mean three-month CD rate	Mean secondary market three-month treasury bill rate		Spread between CD rate and transformed T-bill rate
		Bank discount basis	Simple interest basis	
1964	3.90	3.54	3.57	0.33
1965	4.34	3.95	3.99	0.35
1966	5.47	4.85	4.91	0.56
1967	5.02	4.30	4.35	0.67
1968	5.86	5.33	5.40	0.46
1969	7.77	6.67	6.78	0.99
1970	7.57	6.39	6.49	1.08
1971	5.01	4.33	4.38	0.63
1972	4.65	4.07	4.11	0.54
1973	8.37	7.04	7.17	1.20
1974	10.27	7.84	8.00	2.27
1975	6.43	5.80	5.89	0.54
1976	5.26	4.98	5.04	0.22
1977	5.58	5.27	5.34	0.24
1978	8.22	7.19	7.32	0.90
1979	11.22	10.07	10.33	0.89
1980	13.07	11.43	11.77	1.30
1981	15.91	14.03	14.54	1.37
1982	12.27	10.61	10.90	1.37
1983	9.07	8.61	8.80	0.46
June 1984	11.34	9.87	10.12	1.22

Sources: 1964–1981: *Federal Reserve Bulletin* (various issues). June 1984 figures from Federal Reserve Statistical Release G.13.
Notes: The CD rate is a secondary market rate, quoted on a simple interest basis for a 360-day year (Stigum 1981). After November 1977 it is calculated as the unweighted average of offering rates quoted by at least five dealers. Previously it was the most representative rate quoted in a sample of five dealers. All yields are expressed in terms of a 360-day year. Using t to stand for days to maturity, bill rates are converted from discount rates d to simple interest i by means of the formula: $i = 360\,d/(360 - td)$.

cyclical movements in the rate of business failures but movements in the CD risk premiums as well.

FDIC criteria for being classified as a problem bank were revised in 1980 when the interagency Federal Financial Institutions Examinations Council adopted a uniform system for rating deposit institutions. These new criteria may well have eased capital adequacy standards at the FDIC and FSLIC. Consistent with this inference, between 1980 and 1983 the FSLIC repeatedly relaxed its definitions of what it is prepared to call capital and reservable liabilities. Over the same period it lowered the threshold levels of net worth to assets that triggered regulatory intervention by agency personnel from about 5 percent to roughly 2 percent.

In 1984 capital adequacy standards finally began to be tightened, albeit only slightly. Banking regulators raised minimum capital standards for large banks. The FHLBB set a cap on blocks of deposits channeled through brokerage firms for S&Ls whose net worth is less than 3 percent, although it promised to rescue with FHLB advances any institution troubled by the imposition of this cap. It also proposed to assess a 3 percent capital requirement against an institution's future deposit growth.

Lack of Contractual FDIC and FSLIC Responses to Increased Interest Volatility

Contrary to the first of the insurance system's two principal objectives, the threat of widespread deposit institution failures currently looms uncomfortably large. Secular inflation and increased interest volatility associated with the October 1979 shift in monetary policy procedures have not only raised the level of risk at insured institutions, they have markedly changed the composition of risk. Unfortunately these changes in the nature of risk have been slow to penetrate bureaucratic incentives at the FDIC and FSLIC. As government agencies these entities proved ill-equipped to deal adaptively with the risk-taking environment ushered in by unexpectedly disinflationary monetary policies. The October 1979 change in Federal Reserve policy procedures sharply increased the volatility of interest rates across the entire maturity spectrum and destroyed a comforting negative correlation between inflation-adjusted interest rates and business activity that had characterized U.S. monetary policy since the Fed recaptured its policymaking autonomy in its 1951 Accord with the Treasury. As a result interest rate risk emerged as a potentially deadly threat to highly leveraged agricultural, corporate and foreign government borrowers, to banks that financed such borrowers, and to any deposit institution that chooses not to fund the maturities of its various asset holdings with liabilities of similar maturity.

No private insurer could for long afford to hold its coverages, premium schedules, monitoring practices, and claims settlement procedures constant in the face of such unexpected and unfavorable changes in the composition of client risk-bearing. The principal business of every insurer is to price and to manage its net exposure to risk. To be able to price and to control its risk position, an insurer must identify all relevant forms of risk and operate an information system that tracks in timely fashion all changes in the risks it insures.

In the wake of increased interest volatility, profit incentives have forced managers of deposit institutions to set up asset-liability committees (ALCOs) to monitor and control an institution's exposure to interest rate risk. Typically these committees are supported by service groups that collect data, develop planning models, and analyze the portfolio consequences of alternative interest rate scenarios.

Currently neither the FDIC nor the FSLIC adequately calculates the market value of its exposure to interest rate risk. Neither agency has more than a rudimentary counterpart to an insured's ALCO or even a working procedure for measuring the extent to which the funding positions of its clients are mismatched over time frames of differing lengths. Since 1983 both agencies have been experimenting with appropriate reporting forms and computer software. On March 31, 1983, the Federal Financial Institutions Examination Council introduced procedures for monitoring commercial bank exposure to interest rate risk into the quarterly call report. But with interest rates extremely volatile, quarterly observation is not frequent enough. An aggressive institution can use the help of deposit brokers to achieve substantial growth in its deposits and in its exposure to interest volatility risk over much shorter periods. Moreover agency processing of call report data is slow and exposed to serious reporting error. Installation of electronic reporting procedures is almost certain to be delayed by federal statutes that control the proliferation of reporting forms and by political pressure from client trade associations that understandably resist every proposed expansion in reporting requirements. To client deposit institutions any new report is burdensome. Additional reports raise the cost of complying with (or circumventing) existing regulations. They also introduce opportunities for deposit institution regulators to impose unforeseen additional restraints on their activities.

In the meantime and in the face of a disturbing wave of deposit institution failures, deposit insurance agencies are expanding their de facto coverages and conducting the monitoring and claims settlement parts of their business more laxly than ever. Rather than disciplining client institutions into rebuilding their capital accounts to suitable levels, the FSLIC (and until 1983 even the FDIC) progressively lowered its operative standards of capital adequacy. LaGesse (1984) reports that, subtracting accounting gimmicks such as net worth certificates and deferred loan losses, the ratio of the book value of net worth to assets at FSLIC-insured institutions fell from 4.2 percent in December 1981 to 3.2 percent in December 1983. If the same ratios are calculated net of goodwill accounts, the fall is from 3.8 percent to 0.5 percent. Even using regulators' most lenient definition of net worth, he finds that at year-end 1983, forty-nine FSLIC-insured thrift institutions had negative capital.

As threats to client solvency have mutiplied, examiners have continued to focus on book rather than market values of institution portfolios and to concentrate their efforts on traditional sources of bankruptcy risk: the adequacy of client capital positions (measured at book value) calibrated primarily against nonperforming loans, with some recognition of additional risks from management fraud and incompetence, losses at affiliated firms, robberies, and regional economic decline (Sinkey 1979). At the same time Congress has insisted that both agencies maintain a schedule of explicit insurance premiums linked to an insured institution's total domestic deposits rather than to the portfolio risk that the insured's asset and funding decisions pass through to the insurer.

Implicit Pricing
In the past the subsidy to risk-taking established by insurance agencies' zero explicit price for insuring incremental portfolio risk has been counterbalanced by a policy of imposing risk-related regulatory penalties on clients that exploit the subsidy aggressively. This process can be usefully regarded as a discretionary imposition of implicit insurance premiums. An institution's implicit premium consists of the anticipated profits that it is prevented from earning because of insurer restrictions on its activities and balance sheet positions. To qualify for insurance, deposit institutions must open their operations to federal examination and supervision. Agency interference in client operations is designed to escalate with assessments made by government examiners of the riskiness of an insured's balance sheet and operations. For prospective regulatory penalties to serve as disincentives that successfully counterbalance price incentives that tempt clients to take excessive risks, examiners' judgments about the adequacy of an insured's accumulated capital must be well-founded. In turn insurers' ability to impose civil sanctions and to petition chartering authorities to close risky institutions before events exhaust the value of an institution's charter (the value of the firm's option to continue in business) simultaneously gives bite to examiners' criticisms and represents a first line of protection of deposit insurance agencies' accumulated reserves and backup borrowing capacity.

Cumbersome though it may be, as long as all relevant forms of client risk-taking are monitored, this two-element pricing scheme (in principle) can allocate insured and insurer resources every bit as efficiently as a formally risk-rated structure of explicit premiums might allocate them (Buser, Chen, and Kane 1981). But the problem today is twofold. First, deposit insurance agencies have only begun to institute procedures for making implicit premiums responsive to financial-technology, sovereign, or interest rate risk. Second, even if such procedures could be perfected (for example, by imposing minimum capital requirements that increase with the perceived riskiness of a firm's balance sheet and operations), incentives remain for clients to search out new forms of unregulated risk.

Possibility of Incentive-Compatible Insurance Provisions

Currently, extremely low-risk deposit institutions (if any exist) pay unreasonably high premiums for deposit insurance, while high-risk institutions receive insurance at a bargain rate. Contractual incentives could be established that would allow a low-risk institution to lower its premiums by communicating what its managers know about the institution's net exposure to nontraditional forms of risk.

Deposit insurers have not yet tried to offer contract options that would encourage insureds to assist agency personnel to sort them into identifiable risk classes. Federal deposit insurance comes in only one contractual form, which is packaged in only one combination of contractual ingredients. Individual deposit accounts at every government-insured deposit institution are insured in full up to a fixed amount, an amount that Congress has increased at irregular intervals. Deposit insurers do not allow their clients to opt for lighter or heavier forms of insurance coverage. Coinsurance, deductibles, and alternative exclusion clauses are not offered, even though client responses to differentiation in contract provisions could provide much useful information. In principle product differentiation can be used to reduce the costs of underwriting, administering, and enforcing any insurance system (Rothschild and Stiglitz 1976; Hoy 1982; Mayers and Smith 1982). Today with fixed coverages and fixed schedules of explicit premiums, insureds have no incentive to divulge their true risk class to their insurer. As a result low-risk institutions and the general taxpayer end up subsidizing gambles by an unknown number of aggressive institutions, particularly those that voluntarily short-fund or long-fund their assets as a way of speculating on future movements in interest rates.

Deposit Insurers as Equity Investors

In principle ongoing risks from technological innovation and sovereign lending can be evaluated by making minor changes in examination procedures and may be priced by means of implicit premiums. However, as long as interest rate risk remains poorly monitored, this element of agency risk exposure cannot be priced, even implicitly. This means that aggressive deposit institutions can lay off increases in interest rate risk at virtually zero cost onto federal insurance agencies and ultimately onto these agencies' explicit and implicit guarantors. Under current procedures, interest rate risk is shifted to government entities and to conservatively run deposit institutions.

Calculations to be presented in chapter 4 show that burgeoning interest rate risk has sharply raised the actuarial value of FDIC and FSLIC guarantees of client deposits. Properly accounted, these extremely valuable guarantees are equity instruments that make the U.S. government de facto the dominant source of the equity invested in deposit institutions today. In any country and in any era a government has a natural interest in seeing that its equity investments are "well"-managed. Increased government control tends to follow closely behind reliance on government funding. Recognizing this, an unintended de facto nationalization of the U.S. deposit institution industry becomes a progressively credible possibility.

References and Additional Readings

Barnett, Robert E.; Horvitz, Paul M.; and Silverberg, Stanley C. 1977. "Deposit Insurance: The Present System and Some Alternatives." *Banking Law Journal* 94 (April): 304–332.

Boyd, John H., and Pithyachariyakul, Pipat. 1982. "Bank Holding Company Diversification into Nonbank Lines of Business." Unpublished paper. Federal Reserve Bank of Minneapolis.

Buser, Stephen A.; Chen, Andrew H.; and Kane, Edward J. 1981. "Federal Deposit Insurance, Regulatory Policy, and Optimal Bank Capital." *Journal of Finance* 35 (March): 51–60.

Eisenbeis, Robert. 1983. "Bank Holding Companies and Public Policy." In George J. Benston, ed., *Financial Services: The Changing Institutions and Government Policy*, pp. 127–155. Englewood Cliffs, N.J.: Prentice-Hall.

Gould, Julia A. 1984. "The Merging of the Savings and Loan Industry." *Federal Home Loan Bank Board Journal* 16 (January): 6–11

Hoy, Michael. 1982. "Categorizing Risks in the Insurance Industry." *Quarterly Journal of Economics* 96 (May): 321–336.

Kane, Edward J. 1982. "S&Ls and Interest-Rate Reregulation: The FSLIC as an In-Place Bailout Program." *Housing Finance Review* 1 (July): 219–243.

LaGesse, David. 1984. "Savings and Loan Industry Is Threatened by Rising Interest Rates; Mutuals Hit Hardest." *American Banker*, July 13.

McCulloch, J. Huston. 1981. "Interest Rate Risk and Capital Adequacy for Traditional Banks and Financial Intermediaries." In Sherman Maisel, ed., *Risk and Capital Adequacy in Commercial Banks*, pp. 223–248. Chicago: University of Chicago Press for the National Bureau of Economic Research.

Mayers, David, and Smith, Clifford L., Jr. 1982. *Toward a Positive Theory of Insurance*. Monograph Series in Finance and Economics. New York: Graduate School of Business Administration, New York University.

Rothschild, Michael, and Stiglitz, Joseph. 1976. "Equilibrium in Competitive Insurance Markets: An Essay on the Economics of Imperfect Information." *Quarterly Journal of Economics* 90 (November): 629–649.

Sinkey, Joseph F., Jr. 1979. *Problem and Failed Institutions in the Commercial Banking Industry*. Greenwich, Conn.: JAI Press.

Stigum, Marcia, in collaboration with John Mann. 1981. *Money Market Calculations: Yields, Break-Evens, and Arbitrage*. Homewood, Ill.: Dow Jones, Irwin.

Chapter 4

Current Exposure of Deposit Insurance Agencies to Interest Volatility Risk

How accurately an insurance company prices and manages its exposure to risk is an essential ingredient in its ultimate success or failure. Let us suppose an automobile-insurance company decided to charge fleet owners simply by the car. Unless its flat fee were an exorbitant one, one would predict that this company would attract among its clients every racing team in the world.

Federal legislation requires FDIC and FSLIC managers to charge by the dollar of domestic deposits. Then, to protect their reserves, they control their exposure to moral hazard by intervening in the portfolio decisions of client firms. In effect they make flexible use of implicit regulatory premiums to curtail client efforts to take positions in loan and other capital markets that arbitrage the agencies' nonrisk-related structure of explicit premiums. Instead of aligning their insurance premiums with the value of each client's risk exposure, they try to make client risk positions consistent with the premiums collected.

Such an approach places a heavy burden on the extent and flexibility of deposit institution regulation. In a world of financial and technological change, regulatory lags ensure that some unregulated risks always exist. These lags are rooted in the incentive structure under which federal regulators operate. Congress does not want regulators to anticipate future problems to the extent of undertaking politically painful actions that would regularly resolve emerging problems before they became widely felt. To ensure that the electorate is appropriately appreciative of governmental policy actions, regulators are expected to refrain from confronting stressful issues until ordinary citizens at least see the figurative whites of the problem's eyes. Any regulator who strived to be more farseeing than this would be perceived and criticized as hyperactive by regulatees and politicians alike. To offset the effects of regulatory lags,

Figure 4.1 Portrayal of deposit institution reactions to FDIC and FSLIC mispricing of risks

insurance agency personnel typically strive to some extent to counterbalance the underregulation of emerging risks by overregulating traditional forms of risk. This approach is both wasteful and dangerous.

The success of the system depends on monitoring and responding to client innovations in ways of taking risk. During the 1970s keeping up with unregulated risk is where the deposit insurance agencies fell desperately behind. In the 1980s they have begun to measure but not yet to price or to manage three kinds of risk: interest rate risk, sovereign risk, and the risk of technological change in financial services production and delivery.

Figure 4.1 portrays deposit institution reactions to FDIC and FSLIC mispricing of these risks as creating a bomb whose burning fuse threatens international financial stability. More generally the particular risks illustrated represent the set of unregulated risks of every sort.

Probably Congress and deposit insurance personnel will reregulate deposit institution exposure to risks from interest volatility, sovereign default, and technological change in time to snuff the fuse before it ignites the bomb. But by then, pursuit of unanticipated new risks will have lit a series of fresh fuses. To illustrate the dangers inherent in the regulatory lags to which the current system exposes us, this chapter presents some estimates of how severely interest volatility risk affected FDIC and FSLIC reserves between 1980 and 1982. It also discusses alternative ways in which agency exposure to this form of risk could be brought back under control.

Interest Volatility Risk and Accounting Conventions

Risk implies danger. For a deposit institution interest rate movements are dangerous because they cause assets and liabilities to gain and lose value. Interest volatility risk concerns a portfolio's exposure to the danger of downward revaluation due to future fluctuations in market interest rates. The more closely the yield on an asset or liability keeps up with changes in market yields, the more interest sensitive that portfolio component is said to be. An institution's overall exposure to interest volatility risk stems from imbalance in the interest sensitivity of the individual assets and liabilities it holds when aggregated across a deposit institution's balance sheet. Whenever fluctuations in interest rates cause the value of an institution's asset side to change more or less extensively than the value of its liability side, the institution is exposed to interest volatility risk.

Since 1938 U.S. deposit institutions have seldom recorded portfolio revaluations as they occur. But accounting conventions that preserve book values in no way reduce an institution's exposure to interest volatility risk. They merely shift the dates at which losses are recognized. In an opportunity-cost sense, portfolio revaluations occur whenever interest rates change, even for portfolios that are not formally marked to market. Practical people sometimes argue that these losses exist only on paper, holding that all capital losses disappear at maturity and may be eliminated even sooner by reverse movements in interest rates. To see the misconception, we have only to ask how many of the same practical people would accept bonds that a customer bought for $1,000 as fully collateralizing a $1,000 loan even after increases in interest rates had pushed the current market value of these bonds down to $500. The acquisition cost of an asset is relevant only because the tax code treats paper gains and losses differently from realized gains and losses. Taxes aside, the main effect of an accounting scheme that refuses to recognize capital losses as they occur is to smooth the time path of yields recorded for the portfolio in question.

For example, suppose the market interest rate applicable to a particular bond suddenly rises from 10 percent to 10.50 percent and then remains constant. This yield movement indicates that the market price of this bond has declined. Every institution that immediately writes down its current holdings of these bonds to their new market value will show an immediate loss and go on to record future interest income at the market rate of 10.50 percent. Any accounting scheme that maintains an unchanged book value for these bonds in the face of the decline in their market price defers recognition of the loss and instead spreads it over time as a charge against future earnings. This effectively amortizes the downward revaluation, forcing the reduction in market value to show up as a reduction in the rate at which future income accrues. Such portfolios continue to record the now-below-market accounting rate of return of 10 percent. Hence gaps between current interest rates and accounting yields reported by deposit institutions indicate the existence and extent of unrealized capital losses or gains.

Displacement of past declines in asset prices into below-market current rates of return shows up clearly in accounting reports of the mortgage yields earned by MSBs and S&Ls. Each year since 1966 these institutions have recorded below-market returns on these assets. This record of subpar earnings reflects their longstanding strategy, in an era when market interest rates were secularly rising, of funding fixed-rate, long-term mortgages with short-term liabilities.

Measured against the hypothetical cash flow necessary to keep the market value of a collection of seasoned mortgages from depreciating below its book value, unexpected increases in mortgage interest rates have the same effect as if past mortgagors were to default on a parallel fraction of contractual interest payments. Tables 4.1 and 4.2 construct year-by-year estimates of a variable called the cumulative pseudo-default rate on mortgages held by each type of thrift between 1965 and 1981.

Table 4.1 Pseudo-Default rates on aggregate mortgage holdings of insured mutual savings banks, 1965–1983

Year	(1) Average effective yield on book value of mortgages (percent per annum)	(2) FHLBB series of effective interest rates on new homes (percent per annum)	(3) Proportionate shortfall in mortgage income yield (pseudo-default rate) (percent)
1965	5.27	5.81	9.23
1966	5.34	6.25	14.56
1967	5.44	6.46	15.85
1968	5.59	6.97	19.86
1969	5.77	7.81	26.12
1970	5.96	8.45	29.47
1971	6.26	7.74	19.12
1972	6.53	7.60	14.08
1973	6.77	7.95	14.84
1974	6.96	8.92	21.96
1975	7.22	9.01	19.83
1976	7.43	8.99	17.34
1977	7.62	9.01	15.42
1978	7.94	9.54	16.77
1979	8.28	10.77	23.12
1980	8.59	12.65	32.09
1981	8.97	14.74	39.15
1982	9.20	15.12	39.15
1983	9.72	12.66	23.22

Source: FHLBB mortgage interest rates reported in *Federal Reserve Bulletin* (monthly) and 1982 and 1983 *Statistics on Banking*. (The 1983 figures were supplied by FDIC staff over the telephone in advance of publication.) Average mortgage loans, total assets, and net worth are reported in FDIC *Annual Report* (various issues).
Note: Averages for pre-1971 items are based on four consecutive call dates beginning with the end of the previous year and ending with the fall call for the current year; from 1971 the figures reported average values for the end of the previous year with values for the middle and end of the current year. Average effective yield is calculated as the ratio of mortgage income (net of deductions for service fees) to average holdings of mortgages. Pseudo-default rates are calculated as the difference between unity and the ratio of the entry in column 1 to the corresponding entry in column 2.

Table 4.2 Calculated yields and cumulative pseudo-default rates on aggregate mortgage holdings of insured S&Ls, 1965–1983

Year	Average effective annual yield on book value of mortgage holdings of insured S&Ls (percent per annum)	FHLBB series of effective mortgage interest rates on new homes (percent per annum)	Proportionate shortfall in mortgage income yield (pseudo-default rate on S&L mortgage loans) (percent)
1965	5.59	5.81	3.79
1966	5.82	6.25	6.88
1967	5.74	6.46	11.15
1968	5.84	6.97	16.21
1969	6.05	7.81	22.54
1970	6.16	8.45	27.10
1971	6.17	7.74	20.28
1972	6.31	7.60	16.97
1973	6.72	7.95	15.47
1974	7.07	8.92	20.74
1975	7.10	9.01	21.20
1976	7.20	8.99	19.91
1977	7.35	9.01	18.42
1978	7.72	9.54	19.08
1979	8.21	10.77	23.77
1980	8.80	12.65	30.43
1981	9.58	14.74	35.01
1982 (old)[a]	10.27	15.12	32.08
1982 (new)[a]	10.79	15.12	28.64
1983 (old)[a]	9.36	12.66	26.07
1983 (new)[a]	10.05	12.66	20.62

Source: Effective annual yields are calculated from income and balance sheet data in U.S. Federal Home Loan Bank Board, *Combined Financial Satements: FSLIC-Insured Savings and Loan Associations* (annual). FHLBB mortgage interest rates are reported in *Federal Reserve Bulletin* (monthly). This rate consists of the contract rate plus fees and charges amortized over a ten-year period. Pseudo-default rates are calculated as the difference between unity and the ratio of the figures in column 1 to the corresponding entry in column 2.

a. Two figures are reported for the average effective yield on S&L mortgages because a July 1982 regulatory reclassification of some liabilities as deductions from assets lowered reported mortgage balances and raised effective yields at subsequent dates.

The pseudo-default rate summarizes the distance between the stale yields impounded in an institution's book values and the fresh yields it could earn in the marketplace. In the tables the pseudo-default rate is calculated as the proportionate shortfall of the weighted average accounting yield on aggregate mortgage portfolios at MSBs and S&Ls relative to the effective rate on new mortgage contracts reported by the FHLBB. For example, if the market yield were 10.50 percent, an institution that showed an accounting yield of only 10 percent would be said to have a pseudo-default rate of 4.76 percent.

Although the year-to-year timing of changes in pseudo-default rates varies between the two tables, the cyclical and secular patterns are broadly the same. As unexpectedly accelerating inflation and (after 1979) unexpectedly firm monetary restraint drove interest rates on new mortgages to progressively higher levels, institutions that previously issued large amounts of fixed-rate mortgages reported a widening earnings gap. Compared to the cash flow that would keep the market value of a collection of seasoned mortgages from depreciating below its book value, unexpectedly high mortgage interest rates had the same impact on accounting earnings as if contract interest rates were marked to market and past mortgagors were allowed to default on an increasing fraction of the interest due on the mortgage. Pseudo-default rose and fell with the interest rate on new mortgage loans, reflecting the incremental value of the portfolio losses (or gains) that needed to be amortized.

Measuring Average Life of Assets and Liabilities

Differences in the average life of a deposit institution's assets and liabilities determine its exposure to interest volatility risk. Whether or not portfolios are marked to market, for some patterns of interest rate change, interest volatility risk may be shown to be proportional to a convenient summary measure of the potential mismatch between the futurity of the anticipated cash flows generated by the two sides of an institution's balance sheet (Hopewell and Kaufman 1973; Kaufman 1984). This focal measure of the time structure of a portfolio's cash flows is known as its duration. For instruments that offer a periodic flow of interest and/or amortization payments, duration is a more comprehensive measure of futurity than maturity. Whereas maturity takes account only of the date of the last payments scheduled, duration averages the dates of all anticipated outlays and receipts, where each date is weighted by the ratio of the present value of the cash flow anticipated at that date to the present value of the entire portfolio.

When the durations of an institution's assets and liabilities are equal, its overall portfolio is said to be match funded. To a first approximation a portfolio that is match funded is hedged against interest volatility risk. Ordinarily institutions leave a gap between the duration of their assets and liabilities, either because it is too costly to develop the information and to execute the trades necessary to maintain a daily macro hedge or because they wish to bet on the direction that interest rates are going to move.

When the duration of a firm's assets exceeds that of its liabilities, the institution's portfolio is said to be short funded. Its average dollar of liabilities rolls over faster than its average dollar of assets. When interest rates fluctuate, fresh rates will influence the institution's funding costs more quickly than they will affect its receipts. Short-funded institutions have rising-rate exposure. During the time period between the additional life of their assets and the average runoff of their liabilities, they will have to go to the market for fresh funds. Their capital account stands to benefit from falling interest rates and to lose from rising rates.

When the duration of an institution's liabilities exceeds that of its assets, its portfolio position is a long-funded one. Long-funded institutions are exposed to losses from falling interest rates because the average dollar of their assets turns over more quickly than the average dollar of their liabilities. For a while after their assets run off, they will still be servicing liabilities at stale interest rates.

For institutions that report their assets and liabilities at cost or face value rather than at market, rising rate and falling rate exposure shows up after the fact because, after an unfavorable change in market interest rates, it takes time for accounting yields to return to market levels. Since 1965 recorded yields on thrift institution mortgages have sunk far below fresh yields. This occurred because, in the face of an observed secular rise in interest rates, these institutions continued to issue long-term, fixed-rate mortgages and to fund them with liabilities of shorter duration. If the liabilities that financed their mortgage holdings had possessed an average life comparable to that of the assets they funded, reported thrift institution lending margins would not have come under so much pressure.

Data for banks that report weekly to the Federal Reserve suggest that a tendency toward short funding exists at large commercial banks. Even though the average life of large-bank assets has remained well under one year, the average life of some important liabilities (particularly overnight repurchase agreements and purchases of federal funds) is calibrated in days. In May 1984 Continental Illinois was revealed to be a disastrously short-funded bank.

Since 1970 the accounting return on equity has averaged higher for small commercial banks (those with less than $100 million in assets) than for larger ones (Mallinson 1983). Recognizing that many small banks put almost as high a percentage of their assets in real estate loans as thrift institutions do, it is clear that they must have hedged their interest volatility risk in some way. These firms' strong performance in the face of secularly rising interest rates may be attributed in part to institutional realities that make it hard for small banks persistently to occupy a short position in the overnight federal funds market. This encourages them to be net suppliers of federal funds to large banks. It may also be that in the face of ceilings on explicit interest rates on deposits, competitive conditions in the loan and deposit markets in which some of the smallest banks operated did not force them to shift as large a proportion of the deposit insurance subsidy to loan and deposit customers as larger banks did.

Implications of Deposit Institution Short Funding for Federal Deposit Insurance Agencies

Every insurance contract shifts risk from insured persons or institutions to their insurers. In many types of insurance the risk exposure being insured by an individual client diversifies itself away across an insurer's collection of contracts. Some imbalances that occur at the client level net out when they are aggregated across an insurance company's balance sheet. But client exposure to interest volatility risk does not net out across FDIC and FSLIC balance sheets. When interest rates rise, institutions with falling-rate exposure do not distribute any of their gains to the deposit insurance agencies. Nor when interest rates fall do deposit insurance agencies directly participate in the gains realized by their short-funded clients. Insurance agency guarantees resemble a sale of put options. These options permit the agency to take over an institution whenever its net worth falls short of a regulatorily defined standard of capital adequacy. When its options are aggregated across the institutions it insures, the agency ends up holding a collection of put options whose various exercise prices straddle both sides of current bond prices. Because insurers are exposed to making a payoff no matter which way interest rates move, this risk cannot be immunized by occupying a straightforward futures or forward position.

Insured deposit institutions that occupy a short-funded position expose the FDIC and FSLIC to rising-rate risk. Any that occupy a long-funded position expose the agencies to falling-rate risk. Because the clients on the winning side of the interest rate bet reap most of the benefits, it is a no-win situation for the insurance agencies. If rates change, they lose more on one set of clients than they gain on the other. Even worse neither set of exposures is adequately monitored or managed by either agency. FDIC and FSLIC exposure to interest volatility risk can change dramatically without the knowledge or explicit consent of the FDIC's or FSLIC's management team.

The value of insurance agency commitments can be conceived most broadly as the present value of the expected explicit and implicit future expenditures required from the FDIC and FSLIC to keep insured and a discretionary selection of other depositors whole. Although this value can not be observed directly, it may be loosely approximated in several ways.

First, we can look (as we did in table 3.7) at risk premiums that insured institutions have to pay on their uninsured debt. Multiplying estimates of the average per annum risk premium on deposit institution liabilities times the contemporaneous value of insured deposits produces an estimate of the reduction in deposit institution interest costs that explicit federal deposit insurance makes possible. As a first approximation we assume that the risk premium on three-month CDs issued by large commercial banks can serve as at least a rough estimate of the average risk premium on deposit institution liabilities. FDIC and FSLIC *Annual Reports* for 1983 indicate that at year-end insured deposits were $1,268 billion for the FDIC and total accounts of insured members at FSLIC-insured institutions were $579 billion. Applying the June 1984 risk premium to these balances generates estimates of annual interest savings of $15.5 billion for FDIC institutions and $7.1 billion for FSLIC-insured S&Ls. These one-year benefits exceed the value of insurance reserves at the respective agencies. If we view these annual savings as perpetuities and discount them even at a rate as high as 15 percent, the capitalized value of federal deposit insurance in force would amount to $150 billion. This estimate is subject to both positive and negative biases. On the one hand, the explicit guarantee of the first $40,000 ($100,000 since March 31, 1980) segment of each CD and implicit guarantees on additional balances tend to hold the CD risk premium below the cost of fully insuring the balances involved. On the other hand, differences in a customer's options to respond quickly to bad news make FDIC and FSLIC guarantees more valuable to holders of term liabilities than to depositors with funds in passbook and checking accounts. In addition the market may expect adaptive reforms in deposit institution regulations to reduce the riskiness of future deposit institution operations by penalizing currently unregulated forms of risk. However, even if we halve our estimate of the applicable risk premium and assume that future premiums would decline by 50 percent per year forever, this approach would still indicate that federal deposit insurance liabilities are seriously under-funded.

A second approach is to look at the size of supplemental payments that deposit insurance clients have paid implicitly to maintain their eligibility for deposit insurance. Kane (1982) develops the argument that thrift institution payments of positive federal income taxes between 1965 and 1979 and again in 1983 are best interpreted as implicit premiums required to maintain eligibility for deposit insurance. In 1983 and before 1980 insured MSBs and S&Ls neglected opportunities to reduce their taxes that were inherent in the substantial amounts of unbooked capital losses contained in their mortgage portfolios. U.S.

tax law permits a thrift intitution, in determining its taxable income, to deduct losses on sales of financial assets in full during the year they are realized. In every year since 1966, on a consolidated basis unrealized mortgage losses at MSBs and S&Ls were sufficient to eliminate their federal income tax liability. Between 1966 and 1979 the pseudo-default rate on mortgage loans remained at least seven times the ratio of before-tax income to total assets at insured MSBs and S&Ls, which may serve as an estimate of these institutions' tax write-off capacity. Nevertheless tables 4.3 and 4.4 show that insured thrift institutions made positive federal tax payments in each of these years and that these payments exceeded explicit premiums on federal deposit insurance. Aggregating (without reweighting for asset growth) between 1965 and 1980 S&Ls transferred 2.59 percent of their assets to the U.S. Treasury, while between 1968 and 1979, insured MSBs transferred 1.02 percent. Had thrift institutions used mortgage losses to shelter these funds and invested them prudently, their net worth positions would be less strained now.

Why did thrift institutions pay taxes that they could so easily have avoided? The answer is that by not realizing capital losses on its mortgage portfolio, an insured thrift institution could keep its net worth from falling below the level required to stay eligible for insurance. In 1980 effective FDIC and FSLIC capital adequacy requirements were relaxed when industry net worth deteriorated sharply. But during the 1965–1979 period regulators obliged insured thrift institutions to maintain levels of net worth in excess of 5.0 percent. The opportunity cost of having to maintain more capital and a different portfolio composition than deposit institution managers would prefer cannot be less (and is probably considerably more) than the tax payments they could have avoided.

A third approach is to focus on the unbooked losses in thrift institution mortgage assets. The last columns of tables 4.5 and 4.6 provide a rough estimate of the maximum value of the past losses on mortgage loans that are currently being underwritten, respectively, by FDIC and FSLIC guarantees of deposits at thrift institutions. In principle some of this decline in value should be allocated to uninsured creditors; however, the preference of FDIC and FSLIC managements for resolving failures by means of purchase-and-assumption transactions and uninsured creditors' collateral rights and rights of offset greatly reduce these cred-

Table 4.3 Federal income taxes paid by insured mutual savings banks and ratios of taxes to before-tax operating income and to total assets, 1965–1983 (dollar amounts in millions)

Year	Federal taxes	Net income before federal taxes	Average total assets	Takes as a percentage	
				Of net income	Of average total assets
1965	7.4	n.a	48,467	n.a	.02
1966	6.1	n.a.	51,400	n.a.	.01
1967	4.0	n.a.	55,173	n.a.	.01
1968	8.4	203.3	58,872	4.13	.01
1969	14.3	223.3	63,519	6.40	.02
1970	25.3	192.3	65,986	13.16	.04
1971	63.8	407.4	73,662	15.66	.09
1972	108.7	587.9	82,996	18.49	.13
1973	114.5	592.7	90,851	19.32	.13
1974	81.1	398.6	94,427	20.35	.08
1975	66.5	431.9	101,715	15.40	.07
1976	107.8	614.8	114,045	17.53	.09
1977	139.2	820.3	126,894	16.97	.11
1978	171.0	980.0	137,597	17.45	.12
1979	127.0	776.0	145,331	16.37	.09
1980	−74.0	−323.0	150,259	22.91	−.05
1981	−216.0	−1,664.0	155,577	12.98	−.14
1982	−97.0	−1,326.0	156,272	7.32	−.06
1983	54.0	−75.0	162,505	−72.00	.03

Source: FDIC, *Annual Report* (various years) and 1982 and 1983 *Statistics on Banking*. The 1983 figures were supplied by FDIC staff over the telephone in advance of publication.
Note: Before 1971 average total assets are averaged over four consecutive call dates, beginning with the end of the previous year and ending with the fall call of the current year. Beginning in 1971 reported amounts are average figures for the beginning, middle, and end of year.

Table 4.4 Federal income taxes paid by insured S&Ls and ratios of taxes to net operating income and total assets, 1965–1983 (dollar amounts in millions)

Year	Federal taxes	Net operating income before federal taxes	Assets	Tax rate percentages Federal taxes over before-tax net operating income	Federal taxes over total assets
1965	133.63	953.08	124,456	14.02	.11
1966	96.79	756.79	128,885	12.79	.07
1967	93.78	719.25	138,507	13.04	.07
1968	148.50	995.61	147,753	14.91	.10
1969	194.49	1,237.82	156,797	15.71	.12
1970	216.15	1,114.57	170,538	19.39	.13
1971	359.85	1,677.04	199,979	21.46	.18
1972	517.19	2,227.78	236,196	22.71	.22
1973	621.28	2,700.02	264,364	23.01	.23
1974	532.07	2,221.22	287,583	23.95	.18
1975	500.33	2,149.95	329,015	23.27	.15
1976	775.24	3,153.20	381,671	24.59	.20
1977	1,151.34	4,510.10	447,872	25.53	.26
1978	1,485.75	5,720.85	510,754	25.97	.29
1979	1,307.23	5,068.42	566,725	25.79	.23
1980	294.6	791.6	615,314	37.22	.05
1981	−1,490.6	−7,104.7	651,024	20.98	−.22
1982	−1,609.2	−5,880.0	721,364 (old)	27.37	−.23
			686,225 (new)		−.23
1983	421.5	2,379.0	814,620	17.72	.05

Source: U.S. Federal Home Loan Bank Board, *Combined Financial Statements: FSLIC-Insured Savings and Loan Associations* (annual).

itors' effective risk exposure. Moreover as long as a weakened client remains open, the insurance agencies remain exposed both to new losses and to runoffs of uninsured debt.

In 1980 the values of unallocated losses surged well past the value of each agency's accumulated insurance reserve. This surge goes a long way toward explaining the public's sudden loss of confidence in thrift institutions and their insurers. Although assumptions used to construct these estimates may overstate the value of unallocated losses on mortgages, the inference that since 1980 unrecorded capital losses at insured deposit institutions have exceeded the accumulated reserves of the FDIC and FSLIC seems secure.

Table 4.5 Calculated value of unbooked losses on aggregate mortgage holdings of insured mutual savings banks, 1965–1983

Year	(1) Pseudo-default Rate (percent)	(2) Average mortgage loans (book value) (millions)	(3) Average total assets (book value) (millions)	(4) Percentage of book value assets held in Mortgages	(5) Ratio of estimated unbooked mortgage losses to total MSB assets (1) × (4)	(6) Estimated value of unrealized losses on mortgages (millions)	(7) Average book value of MSB net worth (millions)	(8) Net worth after deducting unrealized mortgage losses (millions)
1965	9.23	$36,992	$48,467	76.3	7.04	$3,412	$3,827	$ 415
1966	14.56	40,095	51,400	78.0	11.36	5,837	4,045	−1,792
1967	15.85	42,794	55,173	77.6	12.30	6,784	4,194	−2,590
1968	19.86	45,566	58,872	77.4	15.37	9,049	4,346	−4,703
1969	26.12	48,091	63,519	75.7	19.78	12,564	4,592	−7,972
1970	29.47	49,745	65,986	75.4	22.21	14,661	4,961	−9,700
1971	19.12	52,365	73,662	71.1	13.59	10,011	5,236	−4,775
1972	14.08	56,554	82,996	68.1	9.59	7,959	5,695	−2,264
1973	14.84	61,600	90,851	67.8	10.06	9,140	6,257	−2,883
1974	21.96	64,696	94,427	68.5	15.05	14,208	6,668	−7,540
1975	19.83	66,698	101,715	65.6	13.01	13,232	7,060	−6,172
1976	17.34	70,315	114,045	61.6	10.68	12,182	7,641	−4,541
1977	15.42	75,524	126,744	59.6	9.19	11,650	8,391	−3,259
1978	16.77	81,195	137,597	59.5	9.98	13,731	8,901	−4,830
1979	23.12	86,683	145,331	59.6	13.78	20,026	9,559	−10,467
1980	32.09	88,883	150,259	59.1	18.97	28,504	9,756	−18,748
1981	39.15	89,636	155,577	57.6	22.55	35,083	9,069	−26,014
1982	39.15	86,591	156,272	55.4	21.69	33,894	7,867	−26,027
1983	23.22	86,439	162,505	53.2	12.35	20,074	7,774	−12,300

Source: Table 4.1 for pseudo-default rates; average mortgage loans, total assets, and net worth reported in FDIC, *Annual Report* (various issues) and 1982 and 1983 *Statistics on Banking*. (The 1983 figures were supplied by FDIC staff over the telephone in advance of publication.)
Note: Averages for pre-1971 items based on four consecutive call dates beginning with the end of the previous year and ending with the fall call for the current year; from 1971 the figures reported average the end of the previous year with the middle and end of the current year. Average effective yield is calculated as the ratio of mortgage income net of deductions for service fees to average holdings of mortgages.

Table 4.6 Calculated value of unbooked losses on aggregate mortgage holdings of insured S&Ls and of potential equity claim on FSLIC, 1971–1983

Year	Pseudo-default rate on S&L mortgage loans (percent)	Ratio of mortgage loans and contracts to total assets at S&Ls (percent)	Ratio of estimated unbooked charges against net worth to total assets at S&Ls (percent)	Total assets (millions)	Total mortgage loans (millions)	Estimated value of unrealized losses on mortgages (millions)	Book value of S&L net worth (millions)	Net worth after deducting unrealized mortgage losses (millions)
1971	20.28	84.86	17.20	$199,979	$169,710	$ 34,417	$13,096	$ –11,321
1972	16.97	84.70	14.37	236,196	200,054	33,949	14,707	–19,242
1973	15.47	85.39	13.21	264,364	225,739	34,921	16,509	–18,412
1974	20.74	84.54	17.53	287,583	243,130	50,425	17,868	–32,557
1975	21.20	82.48	17.48	329,015	271,321	57,520	19,175	–38,347
1976	19.91	82.61	16.45	381,671	315,288	62,774	21,279	–41,495
1977	18.42	83.16	15.32	447,872	372,434	68,602	24,425	–44,466
1978	19.08	82.93	15.82	510,754	423,544	80,812	28,136	–52,676
1979	23.77	82.32	19.57	566,725	466,510	110,889	31,624	–79,265
1980	30.51	80.07	24.43	615,314	492,689	150,319	32,367	–117,952
1981	35.01	78.25	27.40	651,024	509,450	178,358	27,830	–150,528
1982 (old)	32.08	69.44	22.28	712,364	494,637	158,680	25,334	–133,346
1982 (new)	28.64	68.56	19.64	686,225	470,486	134,744	25,334	–109,410
1983 (old)	26.07			n.a.	554,568	144,576	32,752	–111,824
1983 (new)	20.62	63.39	13.07	814,620	516,358	106,473	32,752	–73,721

Source: Table 4.2 for pseudo-default rates; balance sheet information from U.S. Federal Home Loan Bank Board, *Combined Financial Statements: FSLIC-Insured Savings and Loan Associations* (1983).

Note: A regulatory change adopted in July 1982 redefined some balances that had previously been reported as liabilities as contra-assets (deductions from asset accounts). These changes lower the value of total mortgage loans and total assets reported on this basis relative to the earlier basis.

A fourth approach is even more hypothetical. It involves assuming a model of the probability distribution or stochastic process that governs movements in the prices of deposit institution assets and liabilities. Given this model the value of FDIC or FSLIC guarantees to an insured institution may be expressed as functions of the levels of risk assumed. Marcus and Shaked (1982), McCulloch (1983), Pyle (1983), and Brickley and James (1984) exemplify this approach. McCulloch shows analytically that the value of deposit insurance to an insured institution varies directly with interest volatility, the mismatch between the duration of the institution's assets and liabilities, and the institution's capital-to-asset ratio. As Pyle shows, it also increases with the probability that the FDIC and FSLIC will choose for political reasons not to exercise their option to take over the institution as soon as it moves into the money, a probability that is set at zero in the other models. Using his estimate of the level of interest volatility obtaining in December 1982, McCulloch calculates the value of federal insurance guarantees as a function of the size of an institution's asset-liability mismatch and leverage. For an institution whose capital-to-asset ratio was in market value as low as 1 percent and whose asset-liability mismatch was one year, the guarantee would be worth 2.10 percent of its liabilities per year. If these figures for leverage and asset-liability mismatching were representative of the thrift industry as a whole, aggregate guarantees would be worth $15 billion per year. Discounting this value at 15 percent takes capitalized value of insurance guarantees to about $100 billion. Because the subscribed net worth of few thrift institutions is positive in market value, even if the asset-liability mismatch were only six months, the value of the guarantees would remain substantial. The values obtained in this approach prove very sensitive to the stochastic process the analyst assumes. Using a process in which interest rates are less volatile than McCulloch's (a process that is also less well supported by data on movements in asset prices), Marcus and Shaked (1982) construct a model which actually indicates that, for a sample of large banks that includes Continental Illinois, FDIC insurance services are overpriced.

Possible Biases in Procedure Used to Estimate Unbooked Losses on Thrift Institution Mortgages

Pseudo-default rates are meant to proxy changes over time in the difference between the market value and the face value of MSB and S&L mortgage holdings. A pseudo-default rate may be calculated as the proportionate difference between current market rates and the weighted average yield on each type of institution's aggregate mortgage portfolio. Tables 4.1 and 4.2 report annual estimates of this cumulative pseudo-default rate at MSBs and S&Ls for each of the last nineteen years.

Lacking time-series data on the market value of MSB and S&L mortgages, tables 4.5 and 4.6 develop estimates of changes in unobserved capital losses at MSBs and S&Ls from observable changes in the extent to which cash flows on existing mortgages fall short of interest rates on new mortgages.

For MSBs and S&Ls, respectively, tables 4.5 and 4.6 multiply the estimated pseudo-default rates by dollar amounts of mortgage loans and by the appropriate ratios of mortgage loans to total assets. Under market value accounting, this loss is chargeable against insured institutions' net worth.

The procedure used promises to produce upward-biased estimates of absolute and relative values of unbooked losses in thrift institution mortgage portfolios. Although the calculations take no account of potentially reinforcing adjustments for nonperforming loans and unrealized losses in securities accounts, they neglect five important counterfactors. First and most important, the approach neglects the maturity distribution of outstanding loans. In effect the formula we use treats mortgages as if they were perpetuities. The size of this bias may be approximated by assuming an average maturity and analyzing new mortgages and outstanding mortgage portfolios as if they were annuities instead. This conception indicates that the magnitude of the bias would decline with the level of interest rates and with the effective maturity of the industry's inherited mortgage portfolio. Second, some portion of observed increases in interest rates may have been anticipated and priced properly over the expected average life of preexisting mortgage loans. This factor is particularly important in the case of variable-rate loans, whose contract interest rate may be expected to grow or decline on average over the life of the loan. Third, throughout the 1960s and 1970s, interest rates on new mortgages included larger allowances for default risk than interest rates on seasoned mortgages because housing price appreciation steadiy improved equity-to-loan ratios on seasoned loans. Fourth, because of prepayment options and due-on-sale clauses, only a small fraction of mortgage loans remains outstanding until maturity. The life expectancy of a representative mortgage loan lies substantially below its typically 20- to 30-year term to maturity. Data (U.S. Department of Housing and Urban Development, 1980) on the survivorship of Federal Housing Administration loans made since 1957 indicate an 11.4-year average life for 20-year mortgages and a 13.2-year life for 25-year and 30-year mortgages. In future years prepayments received at par may be anticipated to lessen the percentage of mortgage loans earning antiquated interest rates. At the same time mortgage life expectancy tends to rise and fall with the pseudo-default rate because from the borrower's point of view, the calculation expresses the opportunity loss of prepaying outstanding loans at par. Fifth, many thrift institutions had unrealized capital gains on their branch office real estate and often on their term liabilities, inasmuch as secularly rising interest rates cause the book value of fixed-rate certificate accounts and nondeposit liabilities to be overstated.

While relevant, the adjustments involved cannot blunt the thrust of my analysis. Even if I were to halve my estimates of net unrealized charges against thrift institution net worth accounts, after 1980 they would still exceed by an uncomfortable margin thrift institutions' book value ratio of capital accounts to assets. Although MSBs have no stock to price, stockowner-owned S&Ls do. For stock S&Ls to sell at positive market values (as they continually have), the dollar amount by which an institution's unrealized losses exceed net worth accounts must be counterbalanced by off-balance-sheet items. These items may be viewed conceptually as the unbooked value of thrift institution charters, where the term charter is used as a shorthand expression for the right to continue in business while enjoying the truncation of losses conferred by the applicable combination of limited liability and deposit insurance guarantees. When a deposit insurance agency refrains from exercising its in-the-money option to take over a thrift whose net worth has fallen to a substandard level, it relaxes contractual conditions that formerly had served to reduce the value of insurance guarantees to that thrift. Hence the less the market value of the bookable net worth at a thrift that the FDIC or FSLIC chooses not to close or merge out of existence, the more valuable the agency's unbookable guarantees become to that firm's managers and stockholders.

Value of Thrift Institution Charters

Charter value may be conceived as the risk-adjusted present value of a deposit institution's anticipated future after-tax earnings. Under generally accepted accounting principles, sources of value that are not specifically classified are recorded under the heading of goodwill. Such sources would include the benefits of a thrift's reputation for fair dealing and its network of contacts in the local real estate community. It would also include the capitalized value of any net costs or benefits derived from regulation. Net regulatory benefits may exist because the FHLBB, which oversees the FSLIC, is required by law to serve as a friendly regulator. Although not legally required to represent clients' needs, the FDIC is responsive to the political pressure its clients can generate. Although often only temporarily, thrift institution charter values appear to be enhanced by policies regarding (1) entry regulation, (2) lingering deposit rate regulation, (3) FHLB advances, and (4) the pricing and administration of federal deposit insurance.

For any thrift institution whose bookable net worth is negative, the value of federal deposit insurance is substantial. It funds cumulative past losses and simultaneously underwrites the institution's exposure to ongoing risks. It is clear that many thrift institutions could not remain in business if federal deposit insurance could or would be suddenly withdrawn. Theoretical models exist that imply that the underpricing of FDIC and FSLIC guarantees is the dominant element in unbooked charter values (Buser, Chen, and Kane 1981; Kane 1982).

For a troubled debtor the economics of a credible loan guarantee are truly glorious. The weaker the debtor's own position, the higher the market value of the guarantee becomes. To show this, it is convenient to use algebra. Let us define the market value of the firm's insurance guarantee as I, the market value of the firm's other assets as A, and the market value of its nonequity liabilities as L. By the balance sheet identity, the firm's market value is $A + I - L$. Once A falls below L, further declines in asset value have little additional effect on the value of the firm. As long as the guarantor permits the firm to continue to operate autonomously, additional losses primarily increase I. Once a firm's managers reach this state, they have no incentive to economize on the firm's risk-taking. Guttentag and Herring (1982) describe such firms as operating in a "go-for-broke mode." As long as they can play with equity funds supplied entirely by their insurance agency, they want to engage in investment plays whose riskiness on the upside is great enough to move A back above L again. Whenever they win such a play, their firm's solvency is restored. When they lose, the insurance agency picks up all but a tiny fraction of the bill.

Federal guarantees were valuable enough to elicit go-for-broke lobbying efforts from Lockheed, New York City, and Chrysler. They figure to be of at least comparable importance to thrift institutions today. How long could an underwater MSB or S&L stay open for business if its deposit insurance were rendered inoperative?

Factoring in increases in the unbooked value of FDIC and FSLIC guarantees puts a totally different face on the unfavorable deposit and profit flows the industry has experienced during recent credit crunches. At such times, even though explicit accounting profits turn negative, thrift institutions earn unrecorded implicit profits in the form of increases in the value of agency guarantees. Moreover they may be seen to have lost deposits during the 1965–1982 period not so much because deposit rate ceilings immobilized them as because they did not want to pay the price necessary to retain the funds of their most interest-sensitive customers, who held their funds wholly or partly in uninsured accounts. The price of these funds was high partly because of market uncertainty about federal politicians' willingness to provide a sufficient line of credit to back up uninsured debt. When the market value of a thrift's net worth is low, this uncertainty requires deposit institutions to pay large risk premiums on their uninsured liabilities. After 1980 fewer and fewer market participants treated CD holdings in excess of insurance limits and retail repurchase agreements and other nondeposit liabilities at insured thrift intitutions as if they were implicitly guaranteed in full by the FDIC and FSLIC.

Focusing on the years 1977 to 1983, table 4.7 summarizes unpublished semiannual FHLBB survey data on the interest rates that respondent S&Ls offered on jumbo CDs (those whose denomination is at least $100,000). To interpret these figures, we must remember that until March 31, 1980, only the first $40,000 in these accounts was fully insured. As the note to the table indicates, changes in survey format adopted in March 1979 make subsequent figures more representative of the average rate paid to owners of jumbo CDs by insured S&Ls than those for 1977 and 1978.

In 1977 and 1978 only a small percentage of S&Ls offered jumbo CDs. Even in March 1979 only about two-thirds of insured S&Ls offered them. Although the percentage of S&Ls offering jumbo accounts has increased steadily since then, even as late as September 1983 one-seventh of insured S&Ls chose not to compete for large denomination accounts of any kind.

On average the differential between the mean jumbo CD rate at respondent S&Ls and the three-month Treasury bill rate is smaller than the mean differential for large commercial banks reported in table 3.7. Given the sorry state of S&L accounting profits in these years and growing popular doubts about these institutions' viability, if S&Ls had pursued this funding source aggressively, yields on large denomination CDs shoud have averaged at least as high for S&Ls as for large commercial banks. Nevertheless the data suggest that since 1982, the average risk premium offered on large CDs by S&Ls has not always exceeded the average premium paid by commercial banks.

S&Ls' restrained use of funding opportunities provided by jumbo CDs suggests that in recent credit crunches, thrift institutions preferred experiencing a net outflow of funds to paying the marginal cost of attracting a pool of interest-sensitive funds sufficient to maintain their portfolio size. Disintermediation occurred because these firms could not anticipate a high enough return on their assets to pay the interest bill that would be generated by competing energetically for uninsured funds. Throughout the 1970s tax incentives tied a thrift's ability to

Table 4.7 Mean risk premium offered on jumbo CDs by insured S&Ls, 1977–1983

Year	Number of respondents to FHLBB survey that reported offering jumbo CDs — 3 months	Number of respondents to FHLBB survey that reported offering jumbo CDs — All maturities	Mean offering rate on 3-month jumbo CDs at respondent S&Ls — 3 months	Mean offering rate on 3-month jumbo CDs at respondent S&Ls — All maturities	Average issuing rate on 3-month T-bills at last auction of survey month — Bank discount basis	Average issuing rate on 3-month T-bills at last auction of survey month — Simple interest basis	Spread between 3 month CD and transformed T-bill rates
March 1977	8	127	5.78	6.60	4.61	4.66	1.12
September 1977	16	141	6.42	6.89	5.98	6.07	0.35
March 1978	15	135	7.10	7.35	6.31	6.41	0.69
September 1978	14	110	8.32	8.02	8.11	8.28	0.04
March 1979	1,050	2,728	10.14	9.47	9.50	9.73	0.41
September 1979	1,386	2,876	11.40	10.21	9.99	10.25	1.15
March 1980	1,593	3,027	16.86	13.82	16.53	17.24	−0.38
September 1980	1,731	3,106	12.13	10.81	10.46	10.74	1.39
March 1981	1,934	3,158	13.46	14.62	12.70	13.12	0.34
September 1981	n.a.	n.a.	n.a.	n.a.	14.20	14.72	n.a.
March 1982	1,987	3,072	14.65	14.59	12.55	12.96	1.69
September 1982	n.a.	2,846	n.a.	11.21	7.85	8.01	n.a.
March 1983	n.a.	2,692	n.a.	9.14	8.68	8.87	n.a.
September 1983	n.a.	2,659	n.a.	9.52	8.73	8.92	n.a.

Source: Mean rates on 3-month S&L jumbo CDs are calculated from computer summaries of Federal Home Loan Bank Board March–September reporting system. Rates for 1977 and 1978 are averaged across reporting institutions. Mean rates for later years are weighted by reported amounts outstanding in percentage point intervals. Treasury bill yields are taken from a file maintained by Edward J. McCarthy of the Federal Reserve Bank of Boston.

Note: Jumbo CDs are those issued in denominations of $100,000 or more.

make tax-deductible transfers to bad debt reserves to the extent of its specialization in mortgage loans, and limitations on thrifts' ability to hold nonmortgage assets led most of them to operate on the asset side primarily as mortgage lenders, while state-level usury laws and restrictions on the package of prepayment, assumability, and rate adjustment options that could be incorporated into mortgage contracts (restrictions that have since been greatly relaxed by federal legislators, regulators, and courts) made it hard near the top of the interest rate cycle for thrifts to project a realizable return on new mortgages as high as the top-of-the-cycle cost of uninsured funds. Despite being burned repeatedly, most thrift institution managers remained willing throughout the 1970s to short fund at fixed and relatively low interest rates a succession of long-term loans that gave a borrower two valuable options: to prepay the loan if and when interest rates fell below the contract rate and to keep the loan alive even after the original mortgagor sold his or her home. If they could not have advantageously passed the interest volatility risk inherent in this loan-with-options position through to the FDIC and FSLIC, fixed-rate mortgage loans would have become more expensive and adjustable-rate mortgages would have become the industry norm far earlier than they did.

Managing Insurance Agency Exposure to Interest Rate Risk Without Changing Premium Structure

Most deposit institutions find it unprofitable to match fund their assets and liabilities. In part this is because deposit insurance pricing currently makes it advantageous for deposit institutions to take an exposed position. But it is also because match funding is not optimal in any case. Deposit institution customers are willing to pay handsomely for the right to obtain three options: the option to move passbook and checking deposits without prior notice, the option to prepay loan obligations, and the option to draw as needed on implicit or explicit credit lines. Customers on both sides of deposit institution balance sheets possess the option to accelerate the maturity of their contracts and/or to renegotiate other contract terms. Such options make match funding an impossibility (Batlin 1983). They leave the effective maturity and duration of associated assets and liabilities contingent on the future course of economic events. When many consumers exercise deposit or credit options at the same time, they can quickly convert an asset-driven operation into a liability-driven one (and vice versa). They can also transform what previously shaped up as a match-funded portfolio position into one with a substantial exposure to interest volatility risk.

This exposure helps to explain why, as interest volatility increased in the early 1970s, well-managed deposit institutions developed ALCOs. Each ALCO's first order of business was to establish an information system that reclassified assets and liabilitites according to their estimated duration. Today advances in telecommunications and computer technology have made it possible to produce accurate and timely estimates of the extent of duration mismatches in any designated sector of their portfolio (for example, in specific foreign currencies). This information allows committee members to meet weekly or even daily to assess their exposure to shifts in the level and shape of applicable yield curves. Drawing on this information, an institution's ALCO establishes a forum in which the institution's top management routinely assesses opportunities for covering or hedging unwelcome portfolio risks in futures, forward, and options markets of various kinds. Every ALCO's goal is to maintain a strategic long period balance sheet structure by adjusting discretionary items in its portfolio to offset movements in nondiscretionary items. It seeks to combine broad control of the institution's overall risk position with sufficient flexibility in structural details to accommodate initiatives taken by borrowers and depositors.

My analysis suggests that FDIC and FSLIC managers might do well to establish and ALCO of their own. To monitor and control their exposure to interest volatility risk, they need a reporting system that can develop accurate and timely estimates of the consolidated short-funding and long-funding positions taken by their clients. Externally this system would focus on developing and sampling a collection of client institutions whose funding decisions promise to be representative of consolidated movement in deposit institution asset-liability mismatches. Internally each insurance agency would have to make two further adjustments. First, it would need to install a software system designed to marshal the data collected to track agency exposure to interest rate risk. Second, it would have to plan to assemble appropriate personnel at frequent intervals—at least every two weeks—to review opportunities for closing gaps that open. Each ALCO's assignment would be to manage its agency's ongoing exposure to interest rate risk.

Discretionary investments undertaken at the behest of the ALCO would establish an explicit linkage between customer-induced movements in interest volatility risk and the agency's operating budget. The costs of hedging interest rate risk exposure (which have long remained implicit) would become part of each agency's explicit operating costs. Under current budgetary arrangements, profits and losses on futures, forward, and options transactions would be directly chargeable against the gross assessment income the agency collects from its clients. Whenever interest volatility risk threatened agency reserves, operating expenses would rise relative to assessment income. Moreover the extent of a developing increase in operating expenses would alert politicians and the public in timely fashion to any need to consider recalibrating explicit and implicit premiums on deposit insurance.

Incentives for Clients to Search Out Unregulated Portfolio Risk

Installing a well-functioning ALCO at each deposit insurance agency provides a way to measure, manage, and price interest volatility risk. This would correct a specific flaw that has the potential within the decade to unravel disastrously the deposit insurance system. But it only loosely patches the fundamental defects in deposit insurance pricing that underlie this incipient crisis. These fundamental defects are the inequitable distribution of net premiums and the vulnerability to client adverse selection that are inherent in any insurance operation that combines rigid coverages with a nonrisk-rated schedule of explicit premiums.

As long as the schedule of explicit and implicit premiums currently set by federal deposit insurance agencies violates the law of one price, managers of insured deposit institutions will find themselves offered a higher price in private asset and liability markets for bearing particular forms of portfolio risk—those that have not yet been swept regulatorily into the FDIC and FSLIC penalty structure—than deposit insurance agencies charge their clients for backstopping such risks. This price differential subsidizes deposit institution risk-bearing and keeps a large segment of the deposit institution industry poised on the edge of financial peril. The only important counterincentive is the cost to deposit institution managers of having to surrender their jobs in the event of failure. Whether depositors are paid off or a supervisory merger is arranged, the high-level managers of a failing firm usually find their careers damaged. For a long while after the failure, they may find it impossible to obtain another position that offers as attractive a mix of salary and perquisites. But because ex-managers often enjoy contracts that include a generous separation settlement payable as long as the firm is not liquidated and because they remain employable, this counterincentive is only as strong as an executive's aversion to career risk. On balance underpricing federal deposit insurance establishes incentives for managers of deposit institutions not only to pursue leverage and interest rate risk but to reach out for new and exotic ways to take on additional forms of portfolio risk.

Some observers argue that managers of mutual institutions should be motivated to pursue these opportunities less energetically than managers of stockholder-owned firms; however, it is possible to argue the opposite case. In deciding how much risk the firm should assume, managers of stockholder firms face a trade-off between risk to their own career and anticipated benefits to stockholders. Because managers of mutual institutions may plan a personally profitable conversion of the firm to stock status following a big win (in recent years federal regulators have been trying to make management profiteering in thrift conversions difficult to effect) or may impound their winnings into salaries and perquisites without having to share them with stockholders, their position closely parallels that of an owner-operator, for whom the incentive to arbitrage the price of risk-bearing services stands out most clearly.

These incentives explain why only a small minority of deposit institutions use interest rate futures to hedge their interest volatility risk and why deposit institution regulators found that many of the deposit institutions that first engaged in interest rate futures transactions sought to create speculative rather than hedged positions in futures contracts.* To cite an extreme case, when the Washington Federal Savings and Loan Association of University Heights, Ohio, failed in March 1980, examiners found not only that (far from using forward markets to hedge its upcoming commitments to make mortgages locally) the institution had taken a speculative long position in forward mortgage contracts but that the size of its position in forward contracts exceeded its ordinary liabilities by a large margin.

Insurance Pricing and Changing Regulatory Strategies

Congress has begun to abandon its traditional regulatory strategy of attempting to divide financial markets among a regulated cartel of specialized financial institutions. Contemporary legislation—the Depository Institutions Deregulation and Monetary Control Act (1980) and the Depository Institutions Act (1982)—directs deposit institution regulators to adopt a less-interventionist strategy of diversification and deregulation.

The power to authorize diversifications of deposit institution product lines has been assigned to specialized regulators for each class of institution. Although the diversification half of the strategy emphasizes adaptations for thrifts, the two acts encourage deposit institution regulators to develop new asset and liability powers for deposit institutions of all kinds. In combination with rapid developments in computer and telecommunications technology, regulatory action is enabling thrifts to become more and more like banks and encouraging deposit institutions of all kinds to expand dramatically their product line and geographic span of operations.

The goal of the diversification program is to unlock incipient earning power on the asset side of deposit institution balance sheets to enable institutions to pay market interest rates on the liability side. Sponsors

---

*Jaffe and Hobson (1979) report on a March 30, 1979, survey of all traders holding gross positions in interest rate futures markets of five contracts or more. The number of commercial banks active in each of the seven existing contracts ranged from one to twenty-four, while S&L participation was negligible except in the GNMA contract where thirty-three associations held 6.3 percent of the long contracts and 2.2 percent of the short contracts.

of the program hoped that thrift institutions would move toward a match-funded position once interest ceilings and a few other regulations that encouraged short funding were relaxed.

These hopes were poorly founded. The diversification and deregulation strategy continues to be undermined by counterincentives growing out of the subsidies to risk-taking established by mispriced deposit insurance. For managers who are neutral about their own career risk, these incentives make it more attractive to reach out for additional portfolio risk than to diversify existing risk away. These incentives pervert the exercise of new asset powers and inhibit deposit rate deregulation by keeping many deposit institutions in a state of government dependency.

In the early 1980s thrift institutions' difficulties slowed efforts by the Depository Institutions Deregulation Committee to relax deposit rate ceilings. Ironically the continued existence of these ceilings increased the need for thrift institutions to issue uninsured liabilities—such as jumbo CDs, external borrowings, and retail repurchase agreements—precisely because uninsured instruments were exempt from deposit rate ceilings. The process crammed larger and larger percentages of S&L liabilities into formally uninsured categories at the same time that the cost of these funds was heightened by uncertainty about the extent of the deposit insurance agencies' and Treasury's de facto willingness to maintain their previous policy of implicitly backstopping these instruments.

Affordability of Risk-Rated Insurance Premiums

Sometimes it is asserted that deposit insurance premiums are too high (Miller 1981). I have argued that premiums are high only for conservatively managed institutions, whose managers have the power to rebalance the bargain and face market pressure to exploit this opportunity. Managers of stockholder-owned institutions that do not exploit deposit insurance subsidies must contend with the threat of a stockholder revolt or a takeover bid from an unfriendly source. Managers of mutual institutions may demand higher salaries and perquisites and may even convert their firm to stockownership as a way of liquifying the capitalized value of future deposit insurance subsidies.

For institutions that aggressively select risks to exploit the underpricing of yet-to-be-regulated forms of risk—and therefore for the depository system as a whole—portfolio risk is seriously underpriced. Properly risk-rated premiums would simultaneously raise premiums for institutions that have already arbitraged the existing schedule of deposit insurance coverages and premiums and lower them for other customers.

Focusing particularly on thrift institutions, their long-term earnings prospects and their corresponding capacity to service higher premiums may be less squeezed than accounting earnings would suggest. The record deposit outflows and declines in bookable net worth that the industry posted in the early 1980s were offset in large part by unbookable increases in the value of FDIC and FSLIC guarantees. Although accounting losses reflect predominantly the effect of unsuccessful past speculation on the future course of interest rates, some of the deterioration in thrift institution cash flows is voluntary. First, to persuade borrowers to accept variable-rate loans (to reduce thrifts' exposure to interest volatility risk), many thrift institutions in 1981 and 1982 chose lower initial contract rates with correspondingly lower current cash flows. Second, thrifts were less reluctant than in earlier bouts of disintermediation to realize unbooked losses on mortgage assets. Prior to 1980 the FDIC and FSLIC disciplined insured institutions that allowed the book value of their net worth to fall below agency-determined percentages of total assets. In 1980 these capital adequacy standards were relaxed. In September 1981 the FHLBB widened S&Ls' access to tax write-offs still further by authorizing deferred accounting for gains and losses on sales of mortgages and securities.

Amortizing capital losses over a number of years allows a thrift institution to raise funds in capital markets by asset sales without writing down its capital accounts below insurance agency minima. Between 1980 and 1982, thrifts that had positive operating earnings took tax losses on mortgage sales. Tables 4.3 and 4.4 show that in 1980–1982 refunds to MSBs from loss carrybacks exceeded their positive federal tax payments. Although net S&L tax payments were greatly reduced in 1980, they did not actually turn negative until 1981, when the accounting markup on their loanable funds also turned negative.

Earning power is hidden not only in unaccounted forms of deferred income, but also in an institution's ability to shift the burden of financing higher insurance premiums to its borrowers and depositors. To the extent that market forces previously shifted the benefits of existing subsidies to borrowers and depositors, revenue will flow back to deposit institutions as these subsidies are eliminated.

Because subsidies to risk-bearing underlie deposit institutions' continuing financial weakness, it is foolish to permit this weakness to serve as a justification for continuing the subsidies. The country doctor mentioned in the first chapter would not want to wait for his wife to catch her breath before starting to treat her. If Congress decides to eliminate deposit insurance subsidies before the system actually breaks down, it will face irresistable political pressures to do so in a gradual rather than an abrupt way. The sooner Congress puts into motion a scheme for managing the transition to a system in which deposit insurance is fairly priced, the sooner the perverse effects of the current system will begin to disappear.

References and Additional Readings

Batlin, Carl. 1983. "Interest Rate Risk, Prepayment Risk, and the Futures Market Hedging Strategies of Financial Intermediaries." *Journal of Futures Markets* 3 (Summer): 177–184.

Brickley, James A., and James, Christopher. 1984. "Deposit Guarantees and S&L Stock Returns: An Option Pricing Approach." Unpublished paper. University of Utah and University of Oregon, March.

Buser, Stephen A.; Chen, Andrew H.; and Kane, Edward J. 1981. "Federal Deposit Insurance, Regulatory Policy, and Optimal Bank Capital." *Journal of Finance* 35 (March): 51–60.

Flannery, Mark J., and James, Christopher. 1982. "The Impact of Market Interest Rates on Intermediary Stock Prices." *Proceedings of a Conference on Bank Structure and Competition*, pp. 520–538. Chicago: Federal Reserve Bank of Chicago.

Guttentag, Jack, and Richard Herring. 1982. "Insolvency of Financial Institutions: Assessment and Regulatory Disposition." In Paul Wachtel, ed., *Crisis in the Economic and Financial Structure*, pp. 99–126. Lexington, Mass.: Lexington Books.

Hopewell, M. H., and Kaufman, George C. 1973. "Bond-Price Volatility and Term to Maturity: A Generalized Respecification." *American Economic Review* 63 (September): 749–753.

Jaffe, Naomi L., and Hobson, Ronald B. 1979. "Survey of Interest-Rate Futures Markets." Unpublished manuscript. Washington, D.C. Commodities Futures Trading Commission, December.

Kane, Edward J. 1982. "S&Ls and Interest-Rate Reregulation: The FSLIC as an In-Place Bailout Program." *Housing Finance Review* 1 (July): 219–243.

Kaufman, George G. 1984. "Measuring and Managing Interest-Rate Risk: A Primer." *Economic Perspectives* 8 (January–February): 16–29.

Kolb, Robert W.; Timme, Stephen G.; and Gay, Gerald D. 1984. "Macro versus Micro Futures Hedges at Commercial Banks." *Journal of Futures Markets* 4 (Spring): 47–54.

McCulloch, J. Huston. 1983. "Interest-Risk Sensitive Deposit Insurance Premia: Adaptive Conditional Heteroskedastic Estimates." Unpublished manuscript, Ohio State University, June.

Mallinson, Eugenie. 1983. "Profitability of Commercial Banks in the First Half of 1983." *Federal Reserve Bulletin* 69 (December): 885–892.

Marcus, Alan J., and Shaked, Israel. 1982. "The Valuation of FDIC Deposit Insurance: Empirical Estimates Using the Option Pricing Framework." Boston: Boston University School of Management.

Miller, Randall J. 1981. "Are Deposit Insurance Assessments Too High?" *Bankers Magazine* 164 (March–April): 44–46.

Pyle, David H. 1983. "Pricing Deposit Insurance: The Effects of Mismeasurement." Unpublished manuscript. Federal Reserve Bank of San Francisco and University of California, Berkeley, October.

U.S. Department of Housing and Urban Development. Actuarial Division of Office of Financial Management. 1980. "Survivorship and Decrement Tables for HUD/FHA Home Mortgage Insurance Programs as of December 31, 1979." Washington, D.C.; September.

Chapter 5

Emerging Risks and the Deposit Insurance Subsidy

From the point of view of deposit institution managers, insured banks and S&Ls have experienced the negative effects of subsidized risk taking without realizing many of the benefits they might have hoped for. In recent years as the subsidy to risk-taking inherent in current deposit insurance arrangements increased the aggregate risk exposure of deposit institutions, it did little to increase their average profitability. Although in the early 1980s charter applications boomed for S&Ls in California and for commercial banks in Texas, during this same period few investors have regarded existing banks or thrifts as high fliers. This raises the question of where the proceeds from the deposit insurance subsidy go.

How Competitive Forces Shift the Deposit Insurance Subsidy

Part of the answer lies in regulators' tendency to overregulate recognized risks. Restrictions on the pursuit of particular opportunities for profit serve as implicit taxes that recapture some of the subsidy conferred on other opportunities. Another part of the answer lies in book value accounting conventions that understate returns on industry capital by greatly overstating the value of equity funds invested in the industry. Were net worth accounts calculated as the difference between the market value of implicit and explicit assets and implicit and explicit liabilities, a much different picture would emerge.

Still, the largest part of the answer is that competition by insured institutions for subsidized borrowing and lending opportunities is so intense that the bulk of the subsidy is shifted to borrowers and to funds suppliers. A subsidy is shifted when the institution that formally collects the subsidy is led to incorporate some part (and possibly all) of the value from the subsidy it receives into the price of the good or service it sells. When subsidies to lenders are shifted into a particular loan market, they lower the interest rate charged. When subsidies to deposit institutions are shifted into a particular deposit market, they raise the interest rate paid out.

The hypothesis that deposit insurance subsidies are shifted is consistent with basic economic theory, especially if we assume—as evidence compiled by Benston, Hanweck, and Humphrey (1982) suggests—that financial intermediary services can be produced at roughly constant costs. Moreover this analysis has the collateral advantage of explaining two other puzzling aspects of deposit institution behavior. First, why over the 1973–1981 period did commercial banks extend credit to developing and Soviet bloc countries at interest rates that, adjusted for risk, proved so low that borrowing by these countries outstripped their capacity for comfortable repayment? Moreover why did the number of banks involved in this lending grow so rapidly over these same years? Second, in 1982–1983 schemes designed to confer deposit insurance on issuers of municipal bonds, why did most of the benefits from below-market interest rates pass through to the ultimate users of funds? Profit-oriented institutions do not shade their lending margins merely to please local authorities. They do so only because the structure of market returns forces them into it.

How long it takes FDIC and FSLIC managers to recognize the existence of unregulated risk in innovative contracts influences the likelihood of future crisis. To illustrate the problem of regulatory lags, we next focus on four categories of what were at least temporarily unregulated risks: loans to Latin American countries, financial contracts that allow a client institution effectively to broker its deposit insurance coverage to liabilities issued by nondepository institutions, brokered deposits, and off-balance-sheet activities.

Deposit Insurance Subsidies and Lending to Less Developed Countries

Although the sudden increase in the level of U.S. real interest rates that occurred after October 6, 1979, increased repayment problems for many debtors, I maintain that the root problem in the development of the current international lending crisis is the turning on and off of deposit insurance subsidies to lending to less developed countries (LDCs). Prior to 1982, such loans constituted a politically protected class of subsidized risk-taking for federally insured U.S. banks. Even after 1982, pronouncements by Federal Reserve Chairman Paul Volcker signaled a climate of regulatory sympathy toward this obviously troubled form of lending.

Without deposit insurance subsidies, foreign banks would have held a larger share of LDC loans, because U.S. banks would never have permitted so many countries with so limited a potential for earning foreign exchange to sink so far in debt to them. Nor would so many U.S. banks have taken such undiversified positions in individual country debt. However, if these subsidies had continued into 1985 at the pre-1982 level, LDC debt might still appear trouble free. Finally, if U.S. authorities were not so determined to preserve the book value of banks' underwater debt, U.S. bankers would not have to struggle every ninety days with representatives of one LDC after another to develop a fresh schedule of net repayments.

Before trying to develop a policy solution to the repayment problem, authorities need to identify the true reasons that credit became overextended. Several noted economists—who otherwise conceive of themselves as advocates of free markets—have proposed to prevent future LDC debt crises by establishing an annual ceiling on the ability of an individual LDC to import capital. Supporters of this solution presume that the LDC debt crisis reflects a failure of free markets to work properly. They see the problem as one of excessive borrowing by irrational governments. But LDC debt did not become too large for comfort just because borrowers' eyes were too big for their economic stomachs. Lenders may equally well be said to have engaged in excessive lending on projects offering limited real rates of anticipated return. Bankers know that private and governmental borrowers often want more credit than would be good for themselves in the long run. To declare a market failure, one must explain why borrowers' appetites for debt were not appropriately tempered by the prudence of institutional lenders operating on the other side of the market. An institution's stockholders depend on its managers to follow investment policies that maximize that value of their firms' stock. Economic theory tells us that in the absence of taxes and subsidies, the process of borrower-lender negotiation should shape a flow of capital to LDC governments and corporations that could be repaid out of the anticipated earnings it would produce. At the very least, free-market economists who espouse quotas for LDC borrowing should have their Adam Smith ties repossessed.

Analysis of the flow of deposit insurance subsidies indicates that the fault lies not with borrowers and lenders or with increases in the real rate of interest but with the financial regulatory structure of the United States. It is possible to agree with officials in LDC countries who claim that prior to 1982 U.S. banks virtually forced the money on them by offering deals whose bargain real interest rates were simply too good to be refused. These low real loan rates led LDC borrowers to invest at the margin in projects with correspondingly low anticipated real rates of return.

U.S. banks pushed LDC loans as a way of exploiting a subsidy to risk-taking inherent in the then-current federal deposit insurance system of pricing, coverage, and insolvency resolution. Until empirical evidence developed that LDC lending posed a serious threat to FDIC reserves, foreign-policy considerations protected aggressive LDC lending by placing political restraints on federal regulators' ability to impose regulatory penalties on banks committing a large proportion of their capital to LDC borrowers. During the 1970s, although federal officials whispered to banks of their need to be careful, they loudly proclaimed LDC lending as essential to United States and world economic health (Meigs, 1984). Effectively the FDIC's economic viability was subordinated to a grand national foreign-policy commitment to recycling petrodollars. Traditional U.S. concern with strengthening the economy of the Western Hemisphere protected lending to Latin American countries from regulatory criticism even more effectively than loans to other LDCs.

An Instructive Parable

I can consolidate this argument by embodying it in a story about a team of bank loan-workout specialists representing a consortium of European banks and the Morgan Guaranty Trust. This team was dispatched to Mexico to investigate the status of a forty-story skyscraper on which the consortium had made a large construction loan. When the Morgan's representative, a Mr. Sharp, reached JFK airport, he noticed that the operator of one of the travel insurance booths had made a foolish error. He had posted a sign offering free travel insurance without attaching a sticker limiting the amount of free coverage to the small promotional figure of $100,000 that the company's marketing experts had specified.

Not one to miss a bargain, Mr. Sharp immediately demanded $10 billion worth of trip insurance for his upcoming expedition. As Mr. Sharp walked away, the operator of the booth—whom we may call Mr. Slow—recognized his career risk exposure and called the company's headquarters in Washington, D.C., for special instructions. Officials there directed Mr. Slow to shadow Mr. Sharp for the duration of his trip and to try in every way possible to keep him out of harm's way.

When the team of bankers reached the skyscraper project, the wind was blowing so strongly that no one but Mr. Sharp was willing to ascend among the girders to get a better look at the project. Mr. Sharp (who was an extremely graceful individual in any case) felt that if he could complete the inspection under such adverse circumstances, he would emerge a hero in the eyes of his bank. This would win him a big raise. On the other hand, with $10 billion of life insurance in force, even if he slipped and fell, his wife and children would be enriched beyond his wildest hopes for their future welfare.

Mr. Sharp took a walkie-talkie into the construction-company elevator so that he could maintain communication with Mr. Slow. Mr. Slow (who was deathly afraid of heights) remained on the ground in a great sweat. Almost as soon as Mr. Sharp walked out onto the fortieth story, a gust of wind blew him off. As Mr. Slow desperately ran around trying to line himself up to catch the falling body, he opened walkie-talkie contact with Mr. Sharp. Throughout the fall, Mr. Slow assured the banker that even if he wasn't caught, he was no more at risk than either Mr. Slow or his insurance company.

Stopping the story in midfall clarifies the incentives facing the FDIC today. If its many Mr. Slows cannot catch all of the falling Mr. Sharps, the FDIC and its examiners must try everything they can in the way of emergency treatment to maintain at least the appearance of life. The agency's ultimate concern is to prevent its insureds' deaths from being officially recorded. The FDIC is bureaucratically ruined if it does not keep most of its many problem banks at least *nominally* alive. This explains why the FDIC permits blatantly dishonest cosmetic accounting for underwater loans. It is simply not interested in establishing baseline market values for loans to troubled industries and to various LDCs. If it were, by arranging a series of well-publicized auctions of questionable loans from the portfolio of assets currently passing into the hands of its liquidation division, it could easily determine these values.

The story doesn't try to explain why political pressures prevent the FDIC from enforcing the coverage limitations supposedly built into the insurance contract Congress compels it to offer. The essence of the answer is that every government agency is required to make trade-offs between the wishes of Congress and its economic interest narrowly conceived.

How Market Value Accounting Could Contribute to Resolving the Crisis

It is obvious that the market has formed a pessimistic assessment of the true debt repayment capacity of LDCs. Peering through the accounting cosmetics and the flow of life-sustaining emergency loans, it has determined that LDC debt is worth only a fraction of its par value. For purposes of argument, let us assume that this fraction is 70 percent.

What should borrowers and lenders do who disagree with the market assessment? The answer is that the optimists ought to be able to buy out the pessimists. Any bank that strongly believes a given country will pay back more than 70 percent of its contracted interest and amortization payments ought to purchase loans to that country from other lenders. Similarly any country that believes it will in fact deliver on its promises in the long run would find it advantageous to buy back its paper at 70 cents on the dollar. Once remaining borrowers and lenders agree on an estimate of what percentage of a contract's cash flows will never be made, how to restructure the loan should become obvious.

Unfortunately for the prospects of resolving the crisis simply, U.S. banks and banking regulators are unwilling to establish a cash market

Table 5.1 Debt and debt service burdens of Latin American countries (in percent)

	1977	1982	1983	1984
Debt/exports	202.9	274.4	288.5	273.3
Debt/GDP	27.9	42.1	54.8	57.6
Debt service/exports	28.2	54.1	44.0	42.7
Interest payments ratio	10.0	34.2	32.2	31.1

Source: IMF, World Economic Outlook (1984), tables 36, 38.
Note: Debt service includes scheduled interest and amortization payments.

for LDC loans. Although between 1982 and 1983 the value of LDC payment reschedulings jumped from $5.5 billion to $90 billion, negotiations have remained focused on payments about to become overdue and on book values. Adding to the accounting legerdemain, many banks have used the opportunity of loan restructurings to overstate current accounting profits by recording artificial refinancing fees.

So far, trading in LDC loans has consisted entirely of interlender swaps of one country's debt for another. Authorities have discouraged cash transactions, claiming that the existence of an observable cash price might force an accounting write-down of LDC loans against bank capital large enough to panic stockholders and large depositors. Authorities' preoccupation with preserving book values is a serious hindrance to the effective restructuring of LDC debt. Accounting cosmetology aside, selling debt back to LDCs at even a penny over its market value would strengthen rather than weaken the seller. Although the lender would realize a capital loss equal to the difference between the book and market values of the loan, the true value of the lender's net worth would rise by the amount of the premium received over market.

Focusing on the book value of underwater debt also overstates the size and difficulty of resolving the crisis. To see this, let us concentrate on the repayment problems of Latin American countries. IMF data reproduced in table 5.1 show that, between 1977 and 1982 the book value of these countries' debt and annual debt service requirements grew dramatically relative to exports and gross domestic product. Although three out of four of these ratios have improved since 1982, they remain higher for LDCs in Latin America than for LDCs in Africa,

Table 5.2 Levels of mid-1984 indebtedness for four Latin American countries (billions of dollars)

Indebtedness to Western banks	
Brazil	67
Mexico	65
Argentina	26
Venezuela	24
Total indebtedness	
Brazil	96
Mexico	93
Argentina	44
Venezuela	31

Sources: OECD and BIS reports; the Institute for International Economics.

Asia, or the Middle East, where ratios are also uncomfortably high. For the top four Latin debtors, reports by the Organization for Economic Cooperation and Development and Bank for International Settlements released in May 1984 put the aggregate dollar value of debt to Western banks at approximately 180 billion dollars (see table 5.2).

It is important to recognize that properly devalued, LDC debt must earn the interest rate payable on voluntary loans. Naturally when LDC loans are valued at par, they appear to return proportionately less than this. To a first approximation, the cash flow from debt that is worth 70 cents on the dollar should cover only about 70 percent of the equilibrium yield on voluntary new loans.

If LDC debts were recorded at market value, LDC debt burdens would appear much smaller. This is because the market is convinced that, one way or another, the real value of LDC debt is not going to be repaid. Either a heating up of U.S. and world inflation will reduce the purchasing power of the scheduled dollar payments, or scheduled payments will in time and in piecemeal fashion be restructured and written down to recoverable values. Although movements in bank stock prices show that the market believes this fervently, banks and federal regulatory agencies are unwilling to take the accounting write-downs today that would be implied by honestly restructuring a large nation's entire debt over a multiyear horizon. Continuing government efforts to bolster the flow of voluntary finance to LDCs and regulators' fear that deposit runs and a collapse of bank stock prices might attend a sizable write-down of the capital accounts of major banks puts major debtor nations in the catbird seat as their overdue payments approach regulators' mandatory ninety-day write-down date.

Quarterly negotiations between U.S. banks and individual borrowing countries determine how to divide de facto the accounting flow of contractual interest among banks, borrowers, and third parties such as the IMF. Given U.S. regulatory policies, it is in everyone's interest that banks formally accrue this interest. However, each country's quarterly negotiation results in an artificial flow of new accounting credits to cover a major portion of whatever interest and amortization payments are due. The average proportion of accruals that is not delivered by a troubled LDC country provides a loose estimate of the de facto percentage that its loans should be written down.

Negotiations on debt rescheduling are an elaborate charade played for naive publics in both borrowing and lending countries. Debtor countries tell their populace how tough they are in forcing concessions from the banks, while the banks and the IMF pretend that they can pressure the debtor countries to follow austere enough monetary, fiscal, and trade policies to permit the full repayment of their outstanding debts at an unspecified future date. But all parties know that the current market value of the debt and domestic political pressure in LDC countries set the limits within which they negotiate. Banks do not need to settle for less than current market value and LDCs will not press their populations past the point where resentment would boil over into a political revolution or a sharp electoral reverse. If lender pressure were working as well as it is claimed, banks could sell LDC debts to willing buyers at values near par.

The failure of Mexico to receive voluntary new financings by early 1984 (as shown in table 3.6) supports this analysis. For squeezing domestic consumption and switching their balance of payments into surplus, Mexican authorities have been rewarded with agreements that stretch out repayment schedules and reduce contract interest rates on uncollectible bank loans. But lenders are not voluntarily making new loans to Mexico. The problem is that the subsidized loans of the pre-

1982 era were put to work in projects whose marginal real yields were correspondingly low. Returns from these projects are far too small to cover the high real interest rates dictated by the current mix of U.S. macroeconomic policies.

No matter how hard the world financial community may squeeze, they cannot extract blood from an LDC turnip. The need for restructuring, though different in scale, is fundamentally the same as when loans to a domestic corporation go sour in a way (as it did for Braniff or Chrysler) that leaves the firm far more valuable to its lenders alive than dead. In such cases lenders have to figure out what cash flows the enterprise can realistically be expected to throw off and to develop a package of restructured debt and equity claims that protect lender interests while establishing incentives for workers and managers to operate the firm effectively. Regulatory debate about payments moratoria and caps on nominal interest rates neglect an important component of lender claims. They fail to allow for the important contingency that LDCs would be able to make contractual payments in full if inflation should reaccelerate sharply. To confront this issue squarely, restructured contracts might usefully index future payments to world inflation rates.

Opportunities for Deposit Institutions as Portfolio Insurance Subcontractors

On October 18, 1982, the Tulsa (Oklahoma) County Home Finance Authority sold $11.3 million in mortgage revenue bonds. Exploiting a favorable ruling by the FSLIC, the borrower was able—by pledging itself to deposit the proceeds through a trusteeship into FSLIC-insured CDs that carried the same 8.75 percent yield and twelve-year maturity— to eliminate the need to pay a default premium on these bonds. At the same time by extracting pledges from the S&L (or federal savings bank) whose CDs were purchased to make an equal amount of subsidized loans to developers of multifamily housing, the borrower was able to influence the pricing and allocation of the loanable funds it raised. Figure 5.1 portrays schematically the structure of these three-part deals. The S&L is the pivotal institution in that its promise to dedicate the proceeds of the tax-exempt issuers' CDs to subsidized loans for approved developers is what links the bond proceeds to the mortgage market.

Emerging Risks and the Deposit Insurance Subsidy 129

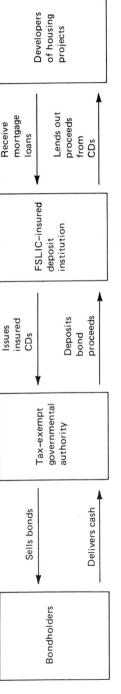

Figure 5.1 Structure of deals that subcontract deposit insurance to issuers of tax-exempt bonds

On the repayment side, linkage is established only between the cash flow on the CD and debt service on the bonds. The S&L's obligation to repay the CDs is unconditional and in no way tied to the delivery of promised payments from the developer-borrower.

During the next two and one-half months, thirty-seven similar bond issues were floated, raising over $650 million in FSLIC-insured funds, two-thirds of them by housing authorities in Texas and Oklahoma. As the device spread to other regions, to other classes of state and local borrowing authorities (such as issuers of industrial development bonds), and to additional investment banking firms, a substantial portion of state and local debt threatened to end up blessed by FSLIC guarantees.

What made the guarantee transferable is that beneficiary interests in a trusteed instrument covered by the FSLIC (and the FDIC as well) are themselves covered up to $100,000 per beneficiary. As long as the borrower's investment banker issued each bond in pieces of $100,000 or less, bondholders could acquire an instrument that is both tax exempt and federally guaranteed.

Interestingly it was the Treasury (which opposes the use of federal guarantees by issuers of tax-exempt instruments) rather than the FSLIC that petitioned Congress to stop the spread of these instruments. The tax reform act of 1984 retroactively outlawed tax exemptions for bonds backed by proceeds from instruments guaranteed by one of the federal deposit insurance agencies. The cutoff date (which was selected when a bill to close the loophole was first introduced in Congress) is April 15, 1983, with an additional transitional exception for bonds whose later issue date occurred pursuant to a binding contract signed by March 3, 1983. Although this particular deposit insurance loophole has been closed, managers of trusteed pension funds, nontrusteed deferred compensation plans, and trusteed money market funds can, by investing in FSLIC- or FDIC-insured CDs, still claim up to $100,000 of deposit insurance for each of their customers. Moreover, they could conceivably link the placement of deposits to the receiving institution's willingness to put the funds into particular types of projects, even corrupt ones.

Because the possibility of packaging deposit insurance for sale to nondepository entities has been demonstrated to be a profitable enterprise, FDIC and FSLIC managers should expect their clients to research additional opportunities energetically. To protect their respective insurance funds, they need to assign agency personnel to the task of monitoring and managing the resulting risk.

Brokered Deposits

Any depositor who wants to circumvent the FDIC's and FSLIC's $100,000 formal limit on account coverage may do so by opening a series of fully insured accounts in a number of different institutions. A depositor who does this without a broker's help incurs substantial shopping and other transactions costs that, in conjunction with deposit insurers' longstanding tendency to rescue insured and uninsured depositors alike, limit the number of different institutions at which it is economical to establish an insured account.

During the early 1980's, as the FDIC experimented with unwinding the affairs of failing institutions in ways that left large depositors and uninsured creditors at risk, the potential benefits to large depositors of dividing the balances across a multiplicity of institutions increased sharply. At the same time, the cost of spreading one's wealth across a variety of insured institutions was reduced by technological developments that permit CD brokers to automate and telecommunicate the process of breaking down an investor's funds into $100,000 pieces. CD brokers have developed computer software that monitors each customer's accounts to make sure that even a very substantial investor would never exceed the $100,000 limit in a single institution.

Deposit insurance guarantees make the insured debt of large banks and small banks (and of sound banks and failing banks as well) into perfect substitutes. CD brokerage services improve the marketability of small bank and troubled bank CDs, greatly increasing these firms' access to institutional funding. But their services also increase the de facto insurance coverage available to large depositors. With roughly 14,000 commercial banks and over 4,000 savings institutions, a deposit as large as $1.8 billion could be made fully insured. Although deposit insurance reform could reduce de jure coverage of large accounts at failing firms, unless the opportunity to use CD brokers to multiply a depositor's coverages is priced or regulated in some way, the effectiveness of such reform would be undermined by the low cost of producing CD brokerage services. Continuing improvements in the technology of electronic record keeping and communications promise to make the costs of managing a deposit account that is broken into $100,000 pieces hardly different from the costs of managing it in an unconstrained manner.

To the extent that market forces shift deposit insurance subsidies backward to depositors, the finders' fee that CD brokers are able to charge deposit institutions are enhanced by deposit insurance. According to industry testimony before Congress (U.S. Congress 1984, p. 131), two leading CD brokers (CDx and Merrill Lynch) charge, respectively, and on an annualized basis, 36 and 25 basis points for this service. In dollar terms this is $250 to $360 for every $100,000 account they can deliver for a year. Given the low unit costs of performing an automated activity, a good portion of these fees may be interpreted as payments a broker earns for subcontracting federal deposit insurance. However, CD brokers are not assessed explicitly for the benefits they derive from transacting in insured instruments.

Broker subcontracting benefits deposit institutions because it provides them with an indirect way to solicit deposits on an interstate basis. By perfecting interregional competition for time and savings deposits, CD brokerage increases transactional efficiency on both sides of the deposit market. If deposit insurance were priced and administered strictly in accordance with economic principles, this would be a wholly laudable result. But because deposit insurance is underpriced, increases in transactional efficiency make it easier for astute customers and deposit institution managers to extract unintended subsidies out of our nation's actuarially unsound deposit insurance system and make it possible to do so in potentially unsustainable amounts. According to the FSLIC (U.S. Congress, 1984), during 1983 the amount of brokered funds at FSLIC-insured institutions rose from $9.3 billion to 29 billion. At year-end 1981, the total was only $3.25 billion.

Brokered funds may be employed most abusively by failing institutions. Managers of failing institutions have virtually nothing to lose by bidding for large injections of brokered deposits and planning to invest the proceeds in extremely risky projects. If these risky projects were to pay off, the institution would be saved. If not, it was going to close anyway. In 1982 and 1983 more than half of the insured institutions closed by the FSLIC had brokered deposits in excess of one-third of their deposits (U.S. Congress 1984, p. 270). The FDIC reports that roughly 16 percent of total deposits in the 72 commercial banks that failed between February 1982 and October 1983 were brokered funds.

Off-Balance-Sheet Activity
In the past deposit institution insolvencies have seldom developed overnight. Even when an insolvency is discovered suddenly (as in a failure triggered by an an examination that uncovers evidence of large-scale fraud or corruption), uninsured depositors have come to expect at least a few days' notice. This expectation is based on two implicit assumptions: that failure is rooted either in a steady deterioration of an institution's balance sheet or in the quality of its loans and investment and that the decision to fail an institution is inevitably a protracted one, slowed by regulators' desire for time to overcome difficulties in assessing the quality of troubled loans and in sorting out administrative options for resolving the insolvency.

Secular growth in what is called off-balance-sheet activities diminishes the applicability of both assumptions. *Off-balance-sheet activities* is the name used to categorize formal and informal commitments that generate contingent claims against an institution's resources. These activities, most of which are listed in table 5.3, may be described as agreements to provide or to guarantee credit and to deliver various other customer services on a standby basis. Because these agreements are offered contingently, generally accepted accounting principles do not require associated claims to be valued and entered on balance sheets of the contracting parties. Although accountants designate associated claims as off-balance-sheet items, economic analysis considers them coequal elements of an institution's generalized or market-value balance sheet.

Contemporary concern that off-balance-sheet activity might trigger overnight insolvency focuses predominantly on risks generated by two activities: standby letters of credit and intraday overdrafts that develop in the course of clearing and settling interbank payments.

Table 5.3 Off-balance-sheet activities

Contingent claims	Financial services

Bank loan commitments, including:
  Formal loan commitments
  Revolving credits
  Lines of credit to customers
  Fed funds and Eurodollar lines of credit
  Commercial paper backup lines
	Loan servicing, including:
	  Mortgage servicing
	  Student loan servicing

	Loan pass-throughs, including:
	  Mortgages
	  Student loans
	  Corporate loans (construction loans)

Standby letters of credit	Trust-related services, including:
	  Portfolio management
	  Investment advisory services
	  Securities processing
	  Customer stock, bond, and money market brokerage
	  Trust and estate management

Commercial letters of credit and bankers' acceptances	

Futures and forward contracts
  Foreign exchange activities
  Financial futures	

Agreements to provide financial support to bank affiliates or subsidiaries	Payment services, such as:
	  Network arrangements
	  Transaction processing
	  Overdraft banking
	  Credit/debit cards
	  Automated teller machines
	  Point-of-Sale systems
	  Home banking
	  Cash management
	  Bank-to-bank payments

Loan participations
  Direct extension of funds
  Risk participations	

Merchant banking that has elements of both contingent claims and financial services such as:
  Private placements
  Securities lending (repos)
  Equity participations
  Corporate finance consulting
  Foreign exchange advisory services
  Gold and other commodities trading
  Tax shelters
  Asset sales
	Insurance services, such as:
	  Credit life insurance
	  Selected other insurance

	Correspondent banking services, such as:
	  Credit services
	  Securities services
	  Trust services
	  International services
	  Payments services
	  Other banking services

Customer leasing that has some elements of both contingent claims and financial services including:
  Tax leasing
  Lease brokering or packaging
	Export trading company services, such as:
	  Export-import consulting
	  Insurance services

Source: Goldberg, Altman, and Furash (1983), p. 9, reproduced in Sinkey (1985).

Standby Letters of Credit In issuing a standby letter of credit (SLC), a deposit institution guarantees the performance of a specific set of financial obligations undertaken by the guaranteed party. By putting its name behind that of one party to a financial contract, the deposit institution relieves counterparties to the guaranteed contracts from having to undertake a detailed analysis of the deposit institution customer's willingness and ability to meet its contractual obligations.

It is presumed that the deposit institution's guarantee is virtually perfect and that its ongoing business relationship with its customers permits it to undertake the relevant financial analysis more cheaply and more accurately than most counterparties could. It is also presumed that deposit institutions would want to screen their customers so carefully that all but the tiniest fraction of SLCs should expire unused.

As Goldberg and Lloyd-Davies (1983) point out, the failure of the Penn Square Bank in July 1982 provides an instance in which all three presumptions proved false. The enormous size of the bank's contingent commitments made it easy for examiners to determine quickly both that the bank was hopelessly insolvent and that a deposit payoff was in the best interest of the FDIC. Even when the volume of Penn Square SLCs is reduced by the value of participations in its guarantees that the bank sold to other institutions, Penn Square's SLCs ran more than twice the book value of its capital, which turned out itself to be grossly overstated (Goldberg and Lloyd-Davies 1983). Worse, the set of energy firms whose loan payments it guaranteed turned out to be extremely poor credits.

Since the mid-1970s federal regulators have required banks to disclose the volume of their SLCs to both federal authorities and stockholders. For purposes of examination and capital adequacy, regulators are supposed to treat these instruments as if they were loans. Even in the face of these efforts at administrative control, table 5.4 shows that the volume of SLCs grew rapidly, much more rapidly than bank capital at issuing institutions. Goldberg and Lloyd-Davies report that the growth of SLCs is concentrated at billion dollar banks. As table 5.5 and 5.6 indicate, these banks (which on June 30, 1983, were responsible for 93 percent of SLC volume) historically have held a much smaller percentage of their assets in capital than smaller banks have.

Table 5.4 Standby letters of credit at insured commercial banks

	December 1978	December 1979	December 1980	December 1981	December 1982	June 1983
Banks with assets over $1 billion						
SLC outstanding ($ millions)	23,410	31,676	42,924	65,751	93,601	99,631
Number of banks with SLC	161	169	189	201	226	229
Number of banks	163	173	190	205	229	236
Banks with assets under $1 billion						
SLC outstanding ($ millions)	2,286	2,980	3,995	5,729	6,596	6,944
Number of banks with SLC	4,112	4,709	5,310	6,079	6,767	7,253
Number of banks	14,215	14,178	14,232	14,195	14,206	14,276
Totals						
SLC outstanding ($ millions)	25,696	34,656	46,919	71,480	100,197	106,575
Number of banks with SLC	4,273	4,878	5,499	6,280	6,993	7,482
Number of banks	14,378	14,351	14,422	14,400	14,435	14,512

Source: Compiled from Consolidated Foreign and Domestic Reports of Condition by Goldberg and Lloyd-Davies (1983)

Table 5.5 Book value of equity capital as a percentage of total assets at insured commercial banks, by size class

Year end	Asset size class					
	Under $100 million	$100–$300 million	$300 million–$1 billion	$1 billion–$5 billion	$5 billion and over	All banks
1970	7.63	7.11	7.08	6.15	5.34	6.58
1971	7.41	6.88	6.83	5.91	5.10	6.32
1972	7.22	6.66	6.43	5.43	4.71	5.95
1973	7.33	6.72	6.27	5.25	4.14	5.67
1974	7.64	6.85	6.43	5.51	3.82	5.65
1975	7.65	6.88	6.58	5.81	4.13	5.87
1976	7.94	7.10	6.78	6.03	4.51	6.11
1977	7.85	6.91	6.61	5.91	4.32	5.92
1978	7.98	7.06	6.53	5.78	4.13	5.80
1979	8.21	7.23	6.55	5.83	4.03	5.75
1980	8.45	7.34	6.77	5.68	4.12	5.80
1981	8.52	7.40	6.78	5.70	4.21	5.83
June 1982	8.75	7.56	6.92	5.86	4.30	5.98

Source: Calculated from Consolidated Reports of Conditions by Samuel H. Talley, "Bank Capital Trends and Financing," *Staff Studies*, no. 122, Board of Governors of the Federal Reserve System (Washington, D.C., February 1983).
Note: Beginning in 1976 equity capital includes the contingency portion of reserves that was previously included in a separate reserve item. If the percentages shown for 1976 and after were adjusted for this definitional change, they would be about 2 percent smaller.

Table 5.6 Book value of so-called primary capital as a percentage of total assets at insured commercial banks, by size class, 1969–1983

	Asset size class					
Year end	Under $100 million	$100–$300 million	$300 million–$1 billion	$1 billion–$5 billion	$5 billion and over	All banks
1969	8.59	8.35	8.28	7.72	6.81	7.88
1970	8.51	8.31	8.15	7.27	6.41	7.59
1971	8.28	7.84	7.82	6.83	6.08	7.25
1972	7.98	7.53	7.28	6.32	5.56	6.81
1973	8.10	7.61	7.15	6.13	4.93	6.50
1974	8.42	7.81	7.34	6.42	4.65	6.49
1975	8.41	7.81	7.47	6.66	4.96	6.71
1976	8.47	7.71	7.40	6.57	5.02	6.66
1977	8.34	7.51	7.18	6.45	4.81	6.44
1978	8.50	7.66	7.09	6.36	4.63	6.33
1979	8.75	7.83	7.14	6.46	4.54	6.29
1980	8.96	7.86	7.36	6.27	4.63	6.34
1981	9.02	7.92	7.39	6.32	4.76	6.39
1982	9.13	7.95	7.37	6.37	4.94	6.48
1983	9.09	7.92	7.36	6.46	5.36	6.66

Source: Compiled from Reports of Condition by Gerald Hanweck, Board of Governors of the Federal Reserve System.
Note: Primary capital for the periods 1969–1975 includes stockholders' equity plus total reserves on loans and securities. Starting in 1976, total reserves was divided into three parts: reserves for loan losses, which became a contra-account netted against total assets; contingency reserves which was added to the equity accounts, and deferred taxes, which was added to liabilities. For 1976 and subsequent years, primary capital includes stockholders' equity plus reserves for loan losses. This definition differs slightly from the definition contained in the Board's capital guidelines. However, complete data using the Board's definition are not available from reporting forms now being employed.

Under current deposit insurance arrangements, all but a small portion of a bank's risk exposure in SLCs passes through to the FDIC and the Fed. A bank normally issues an SLC only for customers it holds to be in good standing. Hence, to put a bank in the position of having a significant portion of its SLC guarantees fall due requires that a number of its best customers fall on hard times. Such an occurrence presumes a regional or national economic decline or corrupt managerial behavior of such a magnitude that the survival of the bank probably would be in question even if it had not issued SLCs.

Per dollar of liabilities guaranteed, banks typically charge at least 50 basis points for issuing an SLC. This fee is well in excess of the 8 1/3 basis points the FDIC charges for insuring a dollar of the bank's own deposit liabilities. The rapid growth of these instruments may be interpreted as evidence that SLCs provide a profitable way for large banks to subcontract their deposit insurance guarantees.

Noncollection Risk In administering customer deposit accounts, deposit institutions take possession of payment orders such as checks and route them back to the institution on which they are drawn. The exchange of instruments between drawee and drawer banks is called clearing. The net value of payments orders cleared by any institution is settled at regular intervals through clearinghouse associations and private and governmental correspondent banks. Unsettled clearings positions with other institutions and with an institution's own customers are subject to the risk of noncollection. Without prior signs of balance sheet malaise, a bank could become insolvent within the course of a single day if its net worth proved insufficient to cover incurable overdrafts executed by insolvent or dishonest customers or if a sufficient amount of the payments orders it has cleared cannot be fully settled.

For two reasons money center banks are exposed to a larger risk of noncollection than other banks. First, because much of the large daily flow of payment orders used to settle bond, stock, futures, and foreign currency transactions clears through these banks, their daily clearings flow dwarfs their capital accounts. Second, in their role as correspondents, these banks perform a large volume of clearing for other banks. Insolvencies at institutions for which a bank acts as settling agent would affect its own net worth to the extent that it cannot reverse transactions it has previously cleared.

Collection risk develops because of payment guarantees and because large customers demand immediate credit for high-value payments (Revell 1983). To limit participants' exposure to collection risk, electronic systems for interregional and international clearing typically limit the universe of institutions that settle directly with one another and provide for same-day (evening) settlement of most items cleared. Because the failure of a large bank to settle would disrupt the entire payments system, most observers hold that the Fed would have to cure the failure immediately to rescue troubled clearing associations and decide how to finance its cure as soon thereafter as possible (Revell 1983).

Noncollection risk is regulated by clearing association and Federal Reserve restrictions on the processes of interinstitutional clearing and settlement. Given that the volume of clearings is growing much faster than the capital of large banks, it appears the Fed's implicit exposure to risks from unsettleable intraday overdrafts has been growing steadily. While the Fed has proposed tighter controls, private clearing associations have already taken action to protect themselves and their members. In October 1984 the Clearing House Interbank Payment System (CHIPS), which clears almost $300 billion worth of transactions among 133 large institutions each day, instituted what it calls bilateral interbank credit limits. In this system each participant establishes a limit on the net amount of uncollected payments it will clear for every other participant. These limits put banks in the unusual position of rejecting (or at least delaying the receipt of) funds from banks that have exceeded the ceilings. CHIPS is also considering proposals for setting up network-wide credit limits and for speeding up the time that promised interbank payments for items cleared become binding and final.

Political Conflict over Deposit Insurance Pricing

Deposit insurance bureaucrats have had great difficulty recognizing and regulating emerging forms of risk in timely fashion. The problem is that government bureaucracies are inherently slower than their clients in adapting to changes in opportunities for risk-taking and are constrained in their adaptation by restrictions imposed by elected politicians. Most politicians want to see the discount window and deposit insurance used as ways to prevent deposit institutions from failing at all during their term in office. Given restraints on their ability to adjust explicit premiums and contract coverages, insurers focus on designing and enforcing rules that encourage clients to adopt safe and sound portfolio policies. In turn deposit institution managers scheme to defeat these rules so that they can convert the discount window and deposit insurance into a source of subsidies. This puts regulators in the middle between politicians and aggressive deposit institution managers. Political efforts to sustain a flow of new deposits to weakened deposit institutions hamper the ability of the deposit insurance agencies to sanction inappropriate risk-taking by aggressive clients. In free markets, weakening penalties for failure encourages unsound management.

Much as forest animals can sense an impending earthquake, more than a few persons who lived through the economic turmoil of 1929–1933 claim that they can sense a coming financial collapse. According to this instinctive assessment, the problems that hit thrift institutions in 1980–1982 and struck banks in 1982–1984 are eating away the very foundations of our financial system. From this instinctive perspective, the principal issue for investigation is to predict through which of several potential points of entry financial crisis will ultimately introduce itself.

At U.S. commercial banks, loan repayment problems surged dramatically in 1982, especially in loans to finance energy exploration, agriculture, and construction, and in loans to Soviet bloc and developing countries. Even optimistic observers fear that new problems will arise and worry about how deposit institutions can afford to offer the returns they have been paying on highly competitive types of deposit accounts. The proper focus for these worries is the ability of the inherited deposit insurance system to withstand additional strain.

The FDIC's and FSLIC's Ultimate Guarantors

What is the capital of Rhode Island?
What is the capital of the U.S. banking system?

Why should anyone want to know the answer to either question?

Political incentives effectively compel the Federal Reserve as lender of last resort to assist troubled institutions in a systemic crisis and compel Congress and the president to backstop explicitly every dollar of formal FDIC and FSLIC guarantees and implicitly even the uninsured liabilities of very large institutions. Once this is recognized, anxiety over the threat of a widespread deposit institution collapse may be seen to be more relevant for uninsured creditors of small institutions than for creditors of large ones and, even at small institutions, for uninsured depositors than for insured ones. Those whose anxiety ought to be most keen are the general taxpayer and managers and stockholders of conservatively managed deposit institutions. These are the parties who in a crisis must expect to underwrite the cost of the Treasury's making good (through higher taxes or higher rates of inflation) the promises imbedded in unfunded FDIC and FSLIC guarantees.

Confidence in incumbent politicians' incentives to protect their chances for reelection makes federal deposit insurance an in-place scheme for bailing out the depository industry. If signs of financial panic were to develop, the president, the Congress, and the Federal Reserve as lender of last resort could not fail to find a way to back up every dollar of insured deposits and most dollars of uninsured deposits as well.

In 1982 Congress confirmed its susceptibility to these political incentives. A bill to set up an emergency relief fund was proposed in February by Congressman F. St Germain. In March the House and Senate passed instead a concurrent resolution declaring that federal deposit insurance is backed by the full faith and credit of the United States. Finally, in late September, Congress gave each insurance agency the authority to issue net worth certificates on such terms and conditions as it may prescribe to client institutions whose net worth accounts amount to less than 3 percent of their assets.

Market confidence in the incentives facing politicians was indicated by uninsured creditors' acceptance after May 1981 of creative forms of FSLIC and FDIC financing. Both agencies engaged in creating pseudo-reserves rather than liquidating assets from their potentially inadequate accumulations of explicit insurance reserves. Between 1982 and 1984, merger assistance tended merely to be promised rather than paid in hard cash. FDIC and FSLIC promissory notes were accepted as equity capital only because depositors continued to trust in the political irresistibility of bail-out incentives. In particularly difficult cases FSLIC and FDIC resources were conserved even more firmly by nationalizing firms and by selling regulatory exemptions from traditional limitations on interstate and cross-industry operation, particularly by facilitating entry for out-of-state institutions into deposit-rich markets of Florida and California.

Deposit Insurance Reform

To assess the odds of a bureaucratic breakdown, we must compare two rates of change: the speed with which the unregulated risks uncovered in the recent past are being recognized and brought under Fed and insurance agency control and the speed with which new forms of unregulated risk are emerging. During the last decade the second speed has regularly exceeded the first.

Ongoing shifts in the technological and market constraints under which deposit institutions operate have cumulatively eroded the traditional architecture of deposit institution regulation. The result is that explicit pricing is replacing implicit pricing in deposit markets. At the same time implicit pricing is being asked to carry an ever-heavier burden in the provision of deposit insurance.

For a world in which interest rates and other business risks are highly volatile, the present system of deposit insurance is unworkable in the long run and unfair. Its unworkability and its inequity are increased by innovations in communications and information technology that make it easier for aggressive institutions to invade the markets of conservatively managed ones.

The essential problem is that politicians cannot permit government-operated insurance funds to concentrate on the economic aspects of their business. To meet political constraints, managers of deposit insurance reserves are forced to compromise actuarial integrity.

Political pressure from troubled clients and insurance agency personnel makes managing the transition to explicit pricing unnecessarily touchy.

Examiners fight against changes that would make their jobs more complex. They strongly resist the implication that in the future they should be responsible for sorting institutions into risk classes that would have explicit pricing implications for examinees (FDIC 1981). At the same time thrift industry spokespersons portray proposals to restructure insurance fees as an exercise in cruelty rather than rationality. Then liken it to kicking an industry when it is down. Trade association lobbyists focus on winning government programs to prevent the liquidation of many of their weakest members. But if these associations' strongest members could be convinced that growing taxpayer resentment could put the long-run ability of insurers to perform the task of backstopping industry liabilities truly on the line, their resistance to deposit insurance reform would prove far less stubborn.

References and Additional Readings

Benston, George; Hanweck, Gerald; and Humphrey, David. 1982. "Scale Economies in Banking: A Restructuring and Reassessment." *Journal of Money, Credit and Banking* 14 (November 1981): 435–456.

FDIC. 1981. "Preliminary Analysis of Variable Rate Deposit Insurance Premiums." Memorandum. (August 31.)

Goldberg, Ellen S.; Altman, Edward I.; and Furash, Edward E. 1983. *Off-Balance-Sheet Activities of Banks: Managing the Risk/Reward Tradeoffs*. Philadelphia: Robert Morris Associates.

Goldberg, Michael A., and Lloyd-Davies, Peter R. 1983. "Standby Letters of Credit: Are Banks Overextending Themselves?" Unpublished manuscript. Washington, D.C.: Board of Governors of the Federal Reserve System, September.

Kane, Edward J. 1981. "Accelerating Inflation, Technological Innovation, and the Decreasing Effectiveness of Banking Regulation." *Journal of Finance* 36 (May): 355–367.

Maisel, Sherman J. 1981. (ed.) *Risk and Capital Adequacy in Commercial Banks*. Chicago: University of Chicago Press and the National Bureau of Economic Research.

Meigs, A. James, 1984. "Regulatory Aspects of the World Debt Problem." *Cato Journal* 4 (Spring/Summer): 105–124.

Revell, J. R. S. 1983. *Banking and Electronic Fund Transfers*. Paris: Organization for Economic Cooperation and Development.

Sinkey, Joseph F., Jr. 1985. "Regulatory Attitudes toward Risk." In Richard C. Aspinwall and Robert A. Eisenbeis, eds., *The Banking Handbook*, pp. 347–380. New York: Wiley.

Talley, Samuel H. 1983. "Bank Capital Trends and Financing." Staff Studies, No. 122, Washington, D.C.: Board of Governors of the Federal Reserve System, February.

U.S. Congress. House of Representatives. Committee on Government Operations. 1984. *Proposed Restrictions on Money Brokers*. Hearings before the Commerce, Consumer, and Monetary Affairs Subcommittee. March 14. 98th Con. 2d sess. Washington D.C.: Government Printing office, 1984.

Chapter 6

Proposals to Reduce FDIC and FSLIC Subsidies to Deposit Institution Risk-Taking

Federal deposit insurance is run as a disequilibrium system. Explicit premiums are calculated as a fixed percentage of domestic deposits. For the marginal dollar of deposits, this leaves the FDIC and FSLIC ready to insure administratively unpenalized forms of client portfolio risk on cheaper terms than the market is prepared to pay institutions for assuming these risks in the first place. To offset the subsidy to risk-bearing that this structure of explicit premiums creates, deposit insurance personnel have to monitor client risk-taking and enforce a system of administrative penalties on clients that they observe to be taking what they deem to be inappropriate risks. The weaknesses of this system are that political restraints inevitably protect particular forms of risk-bearing and that inescapable lags in recognizing the implications for agency risk exposure of emerging categories of client risk-taking reward deposit institution managers for discovering innovative (and therefore unregulated) forms of bearing risk.

Unregulated risks are not only subsidized, they are largely unfunded. The burden of backing up FDIC and FSLIC guarantees falls implicitly on the general taxpayer and on any conservatively managed institution that chooses to resist the siren call of subsidized opportunities for aggressive risk-bearing.

This study argues that generally accepted accounting principles—which allow deposit institutions to carry underwater assets at cost and prevent the value of FDIC and FSLIC guarantees from being booked—routinely distort public perceptions of deposit institution earnings and capital and understate the cost of the federal government's commitment to bail out troubled banks and S&Ls. In the face of an increasingly risky economic environment, the absence of effective taxpayer discipline on elected politicians who permit the market value of deposit insurance guarantees to grow leaves the value of these guarantees out of administrative control. Because the distribution of implicit taxpayer responsibilities for redeeming unfunded deposit insurance guarantees differs sharply from the apparent distribution of the benefits of deposit insurance (which seem to be greatest for the stockholders and creditors of very large institutions), this lack of control cannot be politically sustainable.

Whenever opportunities for institutional risk exposure expand, the deposit insurance subsidy to risk-taking serves to increase the fragility of our financial system. To cut back incentives for voluntary risk-taking, it is necessary not only to reprice but also to redesign the existing system of deposit insurance coverage. The FDIC and FSLIC must develop incentive-compatible insurance contracts and price them fairly. Under current arrangements, low-risk deposit institutions are asked to pay unreasonably high premiums for deposit insurance, while high-risk institutions are offered bargain rates. To limit insured institutions' opportunities for adverse selection, contractual incentives need to be established to allow a would-be low-risk institution to lower its effective premium by communicating the confidential information that its own managers possess about the institution's true exposure to both traditional and nontraditional forms of risk.

I have likened the current federal system of deposit insurance to an old and undermaintained automobile, one that in recent years has been driven at high speeds up and down a series of steep interest rate mountains and over unpaved backroads in LDCs and in energy-exploration regions all over the world. Because it has taken so much abuse, the deposit insurance jalopy is nearing a breakdown and ought to be traded in before it lets its passengers down at an inopportune time.

This metaphor has two instructive features. First, it implies that the largely trouble free operation that the deposit insurance system delivered during its first forty or fifty years is of no current relevance. In ignoring the momentum of the system, defenders of the status quo act like a team of government building inspectors that accidentally tumbled off the roof of a 60-story building. Devoted to duty until the very end, as they fell past the top 50 floors, they loudly reassured each other and the building's occupants, "So far, so good." Whatever good the system has accomplished in the past, politicians and taxpayers need to recognize that its momentum is propelling it in the direction of a bureaucratic disaster. Unless market discipline is reimposed on deposit institution risk-taking, the deposit insurance bureaucracy is eventually going to encounter an unmanageable obstacle.

Second, it is instructive to liken the problem of selecting a new framework for deposit insurance to the process of shopping for a new car. The main question is what features to ask the dealer to install on the new-model insurance system—either immediately or in stages. Options available on both insurance contracts and cars expand secularly. Cruise control, pneumatic shock absorbers, power steering, power brakes, automatic transmission, remote releases for hood, trunk, and gas caps, power locks and power antennas did not even exist in 1933. Systems of risk appraisal, risk sharing, and risk management have improved in parallel fashion. After years of driving an antiquated car, a potential buyer needs guidance as to which of many apparently luxury options a contemporary driver should regard as practical necessities. This chapter's program for deposit insurance reform is conceived as a six-category catalog of optional technological improvements that knowledgeable taxpayers might ask politicians to include on the new deposit insurance invoice.

In an economic environment in which deposit institutions are highly levered and entering new businesses every day and in which interest rates are highly volatile, systematically mispricing deposit insurance guarantees encourages deposit institution managers to position their firms on the edge of financial disaster. Metaphorically, deposit-insurance authorities are paying deposit-institution managers to overload the deposit-insurance jalopy, to drive it too fast, and even to break dance on its hood as it careens through interest rate mountains and over backcountry roads. Reformers' ultimate goal must be to confront institutions whose risk-taking imposes socially unacceptable risks on its federal guarantors with a combination of reduced coverages and increased fees sufficient to move them to adopt safer modes of operation. Their proximate aim should be to make the FDIC and FSLIC act more like private insurers, so that they better protect their and taxpayers' economic interests, treat large and small institutions more equally, and make uninsured depositors and stockholders bear more of the risk inherent in deposit institution operations. This probably involves making much more room for private and even interagency competition in the provision of deposit insurance.

Unfortunately for politicians and regulators who prefer to minimize failures during their term in office, to control deposit-institution risk-taking over the long run, it is necessary to expand opportunities for troubled individual institutions to experience runs and even to fail. Economic analysis indicates that as deposit-institution managers and customers more fully appreciate the extent of implicit or de facto federal guarantees, continuing to rescue insolvent firms becomes counter-productive. In the long run regulatory efforts to prevent de facto deposit institution insolvencies from becoming de jure insolvencies increase the size and extent of de facto insolvencies in the depository industry.

Six-Point Catalog for Deposit Insurance Reform

The adjustment needed must include at least some of six basic changes in federal deposit insurance contracts (Kane 1983). Viewing these proposals as six desirable features available to purchasers of new-model automobiles should clarify that this program is not conceived as an all-or-nothing package. Although the various elements in the package complement each other, adopting any subset of the reforms suggested should provide a better deposit insurance system, one whose operation can be smoothed by installing a system of improved risk-taking incentives.

Market-Value Accounting

The heart of various deposit insurance dilemmas is that a deposit institution's managers have more and better information about the riskiness of their firm's operations than its insurers and customers do. Since 1938 generally accepted accounting principles and regulator-imposed accounting rules have authorized deposit institutions to employ so-called intrinsic-value accounting, which permits assets whose scheduled cash flows are relatively current to be carried at book value. Reinstituting market value accounting for deposit institution loans and investments can be justified as an administratively cheap scheme for raising the implicit regulatory premium on deposit insurance in a risk-sensitive way. The most attractive aspect of this approach is that it makes traditional capital requirements and other implicit premiums more effective, while letting market forces help bureaucrats to conduct regular assessments of an institution's risk exposure and to impose appropriate penalties on overly aggressive risk takers.

That muggers and burglars prefer to work in the dark is reason enough to propose brighter lighting. In a world where declines in market value were not obscured by book value accounting, deposit institution managers who contemplate aggressively pursuing unregulated risks would know that they would have to defend their risk-taking strategies against regulator and financial analyst criticism and to offer correspondingly higher interest rates to uninsured depositors. Moreover, when and if these risks go awry, they would face quicker and more extensive damage to their careers and to the stock price and deposit flows of the institution they manage.

Contemporary accounting principles relieve managers who report book values (and absolve their outside accountants as well) of legal liability for communicating less than their best estimate of the value of an institution's portfolio. Legal authority to use book value accounting to cover up adverse information gives financial institution managers too much discretion over the extent to which current problems show up on an institution's income statement and balance sheet. This managerial discretion puts the burden of valuing deposit institutions on financial analysts and weakens the effect of market and political controls that would otherwise discipline institutions' and insurers' risk exposure. Having to worry about how insurers and depositors might respond to quick-breaking news about potentially injurious developments would establish incentives for deposit institution managers to modify and to bond their behavior in helpful ways.

If private parties are to bear more of the risk inherent in a de jure failure, accountants owe investors in deposit institutions and coinsuring depositors (those that are less than fully insured) a best-efforts estimate of the risk exposure and changing market value of the assets and liabilities that deposit institutions hold on their books. Investors and insurers need reliable information on the value of unrealized losses and gains at financial institutions, information of the sort that conscientious deposit institution managers should be assembling and analyzing in the course of operating their firms. To produce estimates that would be accurate to within a few percentage points of market value, accountants need only to supplement their more traditional bean-counting skills by developing and deploying a minimal competence in asset appraisal. As in real estate appraisal, to value an asset that does not trade, an analyst must rely heavily on data covering current yields and prices in secondary markets for comparable investments. For an institution as a whole, as long as unbiased appraisal techniques are employed, errors in valuing the individual assets in its portfolio should tend to cancel out.

To estimate the value of mortgages and directly placed loans (such as those to troubled farmers, energy firms and LDCs), the major problem is to obtain reliable estimates of appropriate market discount rates to use as inputs into present-value formulas. Practical implementation of these formulas has been greatly simplified by software that preprograms the necessary calculations onto floppy discs or hardwires them into the circuits of hand-held calculators.

If deposit insurers wanted to develop rather than to conceal such information, they could expand the set of transactions observed in secondary markets. Specifically they could request their liquidation divisions to arrange for periodic auctions of assets chosen for their inherent comparability to the most important classes of hard-to-value instruments currently being held by troubled institutions.

Until very recently neither government nor industry has wanted to publicize such baseline values. Although we may cite some tentative administrative steps in the direction of greater disclosure, backsliding continues to occur with respect to politically protected risks. On the plus side, authorities have required banks to report their positions in troubled foreign loans and required S&Ls to report gaps between the interest sensitivity of their assets and liabilities. In 1984 the SEC and Comptroller of the Currency pointedly forced several large institutions to restate their 1983–1984 profits in a less self-serving manner. However, authorities have encouraged cosmetic accounting by permitting problem loans to LDCs to be carried at book value and by promising to take a flexible approach to valuing distressed farm loans at banks located in agricultural regions.

Opponents of greater disclosure offer two objections: that the costs of providing market appraisals might exceed the benefits and that outside parties might dangerously misinterpret the accounting reports that result. Even though market-value accounting promises to increase the costs and complexity of outside audits, it should improve decision making at any firm whose internal information system does not already employ market value data. In addition by simplifying the tasks of financial analysis and of deposit institution examination, it should release roughly the same amount of resources elsewhere in the financial industry. Opponents of market-value accounting worry that it will increase fluctuations in reported earnings; however, by making changes in the portfolio values public, it creates incentives for managers to adopt policies that make the true value of these fluctuations smaller. Moreover, because capital markets must estimate current values in any case, better estimates of portfolio values should reduce (at least on average) the size of allowances that market participants make for the uncertain cosmetic nature of reports of institutional earnings and capital positions. Today allowances for the degree of managerial artfulness permitted under historical-cost accounting depress stock values and increase the cost of uninsured debt even at conservatively managed institutions.

On the regulatory side, market value accounting should help deposit insurers to discover problem situations more quickly and generate popular pressure on authorities to make more timely and better focused interventions. Accounting standards that make it ethical for individual deposit institutions to disguise insolvency and risk-taking beyond all recognition make a mockery of existing capital requirements. Until these standards are changed, proposals to solve the deposit insurance problem by raising or restructuring deposit institution capital requirements can only prove self-defeating.

Expanded Opportunities for Deposit Insurance Agencies to Manage Risk Exposure

To neutralize political pressure for forbearance, deposit insurance agencies need enhanced rights and a greater determination to take timely action on three fronts: to force institutions to maintain the market value of their capital accounts, to cancel the insurance coverage of aggressively managed institutions, or to foreclose on the bank's charter before the market value of an institution's net worth is exhausted. The goal of this class of reforms is to make the current disequilibrium system less breakdown prone by making it easier to prevent institutions that are insolvent de facto from making spectacularly risky endgame plays with FDIC and FSLIC (i.e., taxpayer) money. In recent years so many failing institutions have made last-ditch maneuvers with insured brokered funds that aggressive deposit brokers appear to do a better job of identifying insolvent institutions than FDIC and FSLIC examiners do.

Because insurers may track the same data on CD yields to which customers of CD brokers respond, this appearance is illusory. The jibe has force only because problem situations persist long after the desirability of preserving FDIC and FSLIC insurance reserves should have led the insurer to demand an institution's closure. This delay, which intensifies agency exposure to go-for-broke speculation by failing firms, traces in part to statutory constraints on FDIC and FSLIC problem-solving options. Unlike automobile insurers that routinely cancel their coverage of drivers they deem to be poor risks, deposit insurance agencies lack the right to terminate an institution's insurance on short notice. For example, unless a problem bank neglects to exercise some of its rights of appeal, it takes the FDIC a year to start to terminate its insurance of new deposits, and the process of fully phasing out its guarantees on a bank's existing deposits absorbs two more years. In 1983 the FDIC initiated a record-high twenty-six termination-of-insurance proceedings.

Nor can insurers close an institution they deem economically insolvent. They may, of course, petition the institution's federal or state chartering authority to declare an insolvency. But the interests of this second agency in resolving the problem typically differ importantly from that of the insurer. For federal S&Ls and some federal savings banks, this tension is contained within a single building, as the FHLBB balances the narrow economic interest of the FSLIC against broader political concerns that affect the board. However, whenever an insured S&L holds a state charter, its chartering authority also must be brought into the negotiations. For the FDIC conflicts of interest vary with the character of the regulatory climate chosen by the client. For national banks the primary regulator and chartering authority is the Office of the Comptroller of the Currency. (However, in December 1983, the Comptroller agreed to give the FDIC blanket authority to examine all national banks whose condition falls in the lowest two categories of the agencies' five-point rating scale.) For FDIC-insured federal savings banks the FHLBB holds regulatory and chartering authority. For state-chartered commercial banks that belong to the Federal Reserve System, the Fed is the primary federal regulator but not the chartering authority. This means that to close such a bank, the FDIC must rely on information developed by the Fed and deal both with its state banking commissioner and officials from the Fed.

For the banks it examines itself (insured state-chartered nonmember banks and mutual savings banks), the FDIC may issue cease-and-desist orders against specific practices it deems improper, remove bank officers who engage in substantial violations of laws, regulations, or sound banking practices, and even levy civil monetary penalties. For federal supervision of other insured banks, it must rely on the Fed and the Comptroller of the Currency to take parallel enforcement actions. During the early 1980s the number of such actions has trended upward with the number of problem banks.

Because some of the effects of formally shutting down an institution are irreversible, requiring that an independent agency concur in advance with an insurer's decision to declare a bank insolvent has the benefit of protecting deposit institution customers, managers, creditors, and stockholders against abusive uses of FDIC or FSLIC regulatory authority. However, given that injured parties retain the right to sue for damages ex post, this benefit should be weighed against the costs that delaying the failure of moribund firms visits on the taxpayer. The benefits of requiring the FDIC and FSLIC to win the assent of other federal regulators merely to alter the level and composition of capital requirements or to update procedures for monitoring client institutions are even more questionable.

Insurer rights could be strengthened in many ways. By far the simplest approach would be to consolidate federal regulatory functions over deposit institutions wholly, or at least primarily, in the federal deposit insurance agencies. However, this approach would reduce the bureaucratic dominions of the Federal Reserve System and the Office of the Comptroller of the Currency and threaten job opportunities for identifiable groups of these agencies' employees. Maintaining that their supervisory functions are essential to their greater missions, each agency's leadership is prepared to lobby vigorously to retain them. Because the weight of the Fed's macroeconomic responsibilities gives it extraordinary clout in Congress, the chances of transferring its regulatory powers to the FDIC are miniscule.

Treating the structural partition of federal supervisory authority as a given, Congress has been willing to entertain proposals to increase the authority of the federal insurance agencies to examine insured institutions, to reduce procedural delays in terminating insurance, and to impose further regulatory and civil sanctions on institutions whose managers engage in abusive practices. In the absence of a perceived legislative crisis, however, deposit institutions may be expected to lobby effectively to prevent applicable sanctions and statutory redefinitions of abusive practices from gaining much sweep.

Private deposit insurers ask for and receive much more supervisory authority over actual and prospective clients. Insurance contracts issued by one such firm, the Financial Institution Assurance Corporation (which is owned by its membership), give its president and board of trustees the right to take "any actions" they deem necessary against a member they find to be operating in an unsafe and unsound manner. They also claim the right to require regular and special reports on short notice and may terminate a member's insurance coverage with six months' notice after a 45-day hearing period.

Even without new powers, the FDIC and FSLIC should adopt policies that commit them more determinedly to protecting their economic interests. Not until economic pressure against their reserve funds became severe did FDIC and FSLIC officials systematically begin to take administrative actions designed to foster uncertainty about the extent of their de facto commitment to rescue uninsured creditors.

The most important of these administrative actions was to develop a new technique for resolving failures, known as the deposit transfer or modified payoff. In one variant of these transactions the insurer sells only a failing firm's insured deposits to an acquiring institution and leases rather than sells the dead institution's premises and equipment to the acquirer. In several 1983–1984 failures the FDIC's approach was to sell the acquiring institution only the sum of the failed firm's insured deposits and its estimate of the percentage of uninsured deposits that the FDIC would recover in liquidating the firm's portfolio. If not overruled by the courts, this technique promises to make uninsured creditors take their lumps in liquidation without overly disrupting the financial lives of a failed institution's insured customers. In the long run, I believe that it will prove regrettable that the essentially political advantages of preserving the accounting value of FDIC reserves persuaded the agency against using some form of modified payoff to resolve the multibillion dollar insolvency of Continental Illinois. Whatever the short-run benefits of shoring up the agency's insurance reserves and sharply arresting the spread of depositor pressure to other large banks, destabilizing precedents have been set by permitting an insurer to issue de jure guarantees of both the claims of Continental's uninsured creditors and the debt of its parent holding company.

A second series of administrative actions has focused on reducing the size of the endgame play that an insolvent institution can make between successive examination dates. The goal of these actions is to limit CD brokers' ability to pyramid the $100,000 insurance coverage granted individual depositors to create large blocks of fully insured funds. In early 1984 the FDIC and FSLIC proposed to limit insurance coverage on the aggregate of funds placed in any single institution through any one broker to $100,000. They were forced to backtrack from this initial proposal both by lobbying pressure that CD brokers channeled through Congress and by rulings in U.S. district and appeals courts upholding a brokerage-industry suit against their action. Related proposals under active FDIC consideration include dropping its coverage of any deposits owned by financial institutions and eliminating various forms of trusteed accounts' rights to what has amounted to virtually unlimited coverage. Both proposals are aimed at closing loopholes through which a CD broker could almost costlessly circumvent FDIC and FSLIC efforts to control the proliferation of brokered funds in failing institutions.

On the issue of brokered deposits the FDIC's and FSLIC's only victory so far has been to increase reporting frequencies for institutions that rely heavily on brokered deposits. Beginning in August 1984 FDIC-insured banks are required to file monthly reports and to be prepared to submit to sudden examination whenever 5 or more percent of their deposits comes from CD brokers. This asymmetric data-gathering requirement underscores the inadequacy of the FDIC's and FSLIC's overall information systems. Insurers' information systems have lagged notably behind those operated by large, well-managed commercial banks. As more deposit institutions adopt electronic record-keeping and as telecommunications systems improve, more frequent and more extensive readings of clients' electronic balance sheets become progressively less burdensome. With a more adequate flow of information, ALCOs could be set up to manage each agency's aggregate exposure to interest volatility, industry, and country risk.

Recalibration of Insurance Coverages
The economic value of a dollar of deposit insurance varies in two ways: at a given institution, it varies with the type of account covered, and for a given type of account, it varies with the riskiness of the portfolio policies followed at the institution that issues the deposits. As a complementary way of improving insurers' information flow, Congress should permit deposit insurers to alter their coverages and fee structure to generate information on an individual institution's own perception of the benefits it reaps from insuring different types of accounts in different ways. Insurers and creditors have less information about an institution's risk exposure than the institution's managers have. By developing a wider-ranging structure of insurance coverages and associated premiums, managerial assessments of the value of different kinds of coverage could be extracted from their willingness and unwillingness to pay a set of carefully varied asking prices for specific coverages. Even more information could be gathered if clients were permitted to switch insurers in pursuit of what they regard as cheaper or more reliable coverages.

Managers' selection of coverages signals how risky they and their customers perceive a given institution to be. Low-risk institutions should operate most profitably with minimal coverages. Money market mutual funds provide an instance of conservatively managed near-depository institutions that operate effectively without any insurance at all. On the other hand, high-risk institutions should be able to compete best when they obtain maximal coverages from one or more extremely reliable insurers. If the representative institution were to demand maximal coverages on all account types, we could infer that the price of each type of insurance is too low across the board and that risk-bearing is being subsidized industry wide.

What is needed is a strategy for assembling information on which a reliable process of risk rating could be based. While tactical details must be left to insurance specialists, I recommend three changes in contract provisions. The first change is to lower (perhaps gradually) the basic coverage per account to a level sufficient to protect the transactions and precautionary balances of most household customers. An upper limit of $10,000 is particularly attractive inasmuch as this is the minimum denomination on U.S. Treasury bills that serve as a close substitute for large-denomination holdings of insured deposits. If such a limit is adopted, future values of the ceiling should simultaneously be indexed for inflation to make it more difficult for lobbying pressure to reintroduce the real value of maximum account coverage into the political arena. Congress needs to recognize that its decision to increase account coverage to $100,000 in 1980 was a serious mistake that it should strive to rectify as soon as possible. Fully insuring large denomination deposits effectively permits banks to issue high-denomination, federally guaranteed debt that in divisibility and liquidity is actually superior to ordinary Treasury securities.

The second change is to develop a system for differentially pricing successive layers of optional supplementary coverages (offered, say, in $10,000 slices) and adjusting these prices in accordance with market principles. These coverages could be purchased either by institutions acting on behalf of holders of specific classes of deposit accounts or by individual depositors acting on their own. Market-based pricing would seek to cover the implicit and explicit costs of producing FDIC and FSLIC insurance services at the level of client demand served.

The final change is to introduce provisions for deductible and coinsurance elements into these supplementary coverages. In introducing these elements, authorities could investigate the effects of relating progressive declines in coverage directly to account size and inversely to an account's maturity. A complementary action would be to impose cumulative lifetime limits on the collectibility of an individual or institutional depositor's aggregate claims on the federal deposit insurance agencies. Adopting cumulative ceilings would parallel the coverage patterns employed in underwriting major medical insurance, making it important for even fully insured depositors to care whether CD brokers transfer their funds into insolvent institutions.

Opponents emphasize that these adjustments would penalize large depositors and increase deposit institution funding costs. The other side of this criticism is that existing subsidies are antiegalitarian welfare for rich transactors who can hold large-denomination Treasury debt directly. Taxpayers as a whole would benefit from reducing the true cost to government entities of underwriting deposit institution risk taking.

Risk-Rated Explicit Premiums
Risk rating is the process of analyzing and pricing the risk exposure inherent in a particular insurance contract. Explicit insurance premiums are fees that clients pay in the coin of the realm. The major benefit from realigning deposit insurance coverages would be to produce information that an insurer could use to develop a premium structure that would curtail its exposure to adverse selection. Risk-sensitive explicit pricing is needed to relegate ex ante implicit premiums on previously recognized forms of risk-taking to a lesser role.

Risk-rated explicit premiums need not consist entirely of ex ante payments. Such payments may include procedures for an ex post settling up of gains and losses among an insured institution, its stockholders, and the insurer. Ex post settlement schemes may impose additional liabilities on the stockholders of a failed institution or even on the stockholders of its parent holding company (as in the double or triple liability that used to apply to holders of a bank's stock) or give the insurer the right to sue for a share of any gains that a client reaps from forms of risk-taking that FDIC or FSLIC policy statements declare to have been abusive.

The many opponents of this change emphasize that setting ex ante premiums or designing an equitable scheme for ex post settling up is a difficult task, requiring a considerably larger information base than is collected today (Horvitz 1983). However difficult it may be, it is not beyond the capability of the modern methods of contingent contract writing and information processing. As Pyle (1984) points out, corporate bond markets undertake similar kinds of risk assessments every trading day. Nor are these risk assessments demonstrably more difficult than others that private insurance companies perform. Modern insurance companies price many exotic forms of risk, including damages visited on insured parties by computer crime, divorce, cancer, tax audits, and space debris. No matter how great the practical difficulties of rating a deposit institution's risk exposure, the current approach is defective in principle. To maintain permanently an unfunded system that insures risk borne by deposit institutions at a price that lies far below the return offered in capital markets for risk-bearing services is to establish a kind of Ponzi scheme. The longer such a system remains in place, the more severely it will be tested. As time passes, individual institutions become more fully aware of opportunities for exploiting the situation and develop less compunction about seeking to take advantage of them.

Although ex post settlement is administratively easier than ex ante pricing, the concept frightens many deposit institution managers. They point out that a return to double or triple liability on deposit institution stock would raise the cost of raising private equity capital. They also express concern that FDIC and FSLIC policy statements could degenerate into devices for bringing political influence to bear on institutions' lending priorities. To make sure that these policy statements serve only the purpose of ruling out such demonstrably dangerous activities as betting an institution's very survival on the future course of interest rates or on the success of particular types of investment projects, it would be useful to assign the task of defining abuses to an independent deposit insurance standards board made up of leading practitioners and industry analysts.

What makes risk-sensitive pricing such a hard task is the essential fluidity of opportunities to take risk in financial markets. An institution's adaptive efficiency may be defined as its organizational resourcefulness, which reflects its managers' capacity to think deeply about simple problems and the flexibility they show in adjusting their administrative stucture and procedures to cope with sudden or rapid change. To keep risk ratings and insurance premiums current requires considerable adaptive efficiency. For this reason it seems dangerous to assign the function wholly to government officials. This leads to the fifth point in my program.

Opportunities for Mixed Private and Governmental Competition in Deposit Insurance

To enhance incentives for deposit insurance agencies to maximize their adaptive efficiency, it is necessary to provide opportunities for the FDIC and FSLIC to compete with each other (Benston 1983) and for private firms to issue or to reinsure at least some layers of supplementary deposit insurance coverage. To neutralize political pressure for low prices and uneconomic coverages, authorities must invite into the process of designing and pricing contracts decision makers whose only stakes are economic—parties whose jobs and firms can and will be wiped out if they issue contracts that fail to make it a client's own best interest to keep its risk exposure within prudent bounds.

Private firms can be counted on to enter any business in which they can anticipate earning a fair return. In fact private insurance companies have begun to nibble eagerly around the edges of the deposit insurance market. So far they have focused principally on offering supplementary guarantees for individual accountholders that, beginning where federal guarantees stop, greatly extend the size of the balance covered. Such insurance is particularly attractive to nondepository institutions such as brokerage firms and insurance companies seeking to market newfangled substitutes for ordinary deposits. One notable example is Aetna's provision of supplementary guarantees that operate on top of the Securities Investor Protection Corporation's $500,000 basic guarantee to lift coverage for any holder of a Merrill Lynch's cash management account to $10 million. In a more exotic vein, Cigna Corporation briefly issued Citicorp $900 million worth of insurance against the risk of currency inconvertibility in five countries. The policies covered the contingency that scheduled repayments by debtors in Argentina, Brazil, Mexico, Venezuela, and the Philippines would fail to be remitted because their governments might decide against permitting local currency to be converted into dollars. The contracts included a deductible equal to 25 percent of Citicorp's exposure in each country and a six-month delay before any unremitted debt proceeds may be collected. Affirming the interest of other segments of the industry, Cigna announced that it had reinsured over 95 percent of the coverage with other firms.

While private insurance of deposit institution risks should continue to grow, as long as Congress requires the deposit insurance agencies to maintain unrealistically low explicit premiums, the core of federal insurers' business will remain insulated from the discipline of private competition. This insulation enables agency managers to emphasize political and bureaucratic objectives over their need to adapt economically to rapid change.

Statutory Constraints on FDIC, FSLIC, and Federal Reserve Authority to Rescue Insolvent Large Institutions

Although deposit institution regulators profess a sincere belief in the theoretical benefits of market discipline, practical circumstances inevitably make them reluctant to liquidate a large institution. Given the short terms of office that financial regulators enjoy, it makes little sense for them to take an appreciable chance that a spillover of financial pressure will damage other institutions or undermine public confidence in depository institutions as a whole. Why should an agency's leader risk ruining their own careers when they can reliably truncate further damage with a readily obtained injection of federal funds and federal guarantees that serve to rescue a failing institution and its creditors from the need to sustain uncomfortable levels of losses? Confirming this analysis, Comptroller of the Currency Todd Conover went so far as to assert that in September 1984 the federal government would not allow any of the nation's eleven largest banks to be liquidated.

To hear the sirens' song without being lured to his death, Ulysses had to arrange to have himself strapped to the mast of his ship. Similarly, the reliable way to lessen the probability that the Fed and federal deposit insurers will routinely bail out large, insolvent deposit institutions and (potentially) private deposit insurance companies is to place statutory limits on their ability to respond to the political and bureaucratic siren call of short-sighted opportunities for using federal resources to rescue firms that are insolvent de facto.

Although any proposal to limit the discretion of deposit institution regulators is bound to be controversial, the potential for private loss must be strengthened if implicit federal guarantees are to be made imperfect enough for market discipline to operate properly. The first and most important step would be to require that federal deposit insurance agencies (like private deposit insurers) leave the short-term responsibility for stabilizing the financial system wholly in the hands of the Federal Reserve, acting in its capacity as lender of last resort. Deposit insurance will not be properly priced as long as bailout responsibilities compromise the economic function of deposit insurance reserves. Responsibility for stabilizing financial markets should not be crammed into the mission statement of federal deposit insurance agencies. Second, even the Federal Reserve's capacity for bailing out insolvent institutions needs to be constrained. Except in the event of a bona fide crisis—as defined by the condition that a given percentage (say, at least 5 percent) of aggregate deposit institution assets has been involved in de jure failures within the last twelve or eighteen months—the Fed should not be allowed to lend funds to an institution whose net worth is negative in market value. This would increase the probability that one or two large institutions could fail de jure but leave the Fed free both to assist a troubled firm to arrange financing from private sources and to arrest a developing run on the system as a whole.

What this reform would not do is to let authorities repeatedly use the mere possibility of a systemic run as a justification for bailing out individual institutions as a matter of course. The policy of routinely bailing out financially devastated institutions imposes enormous unaccounted expense and unrecognized liabilities onto the deposit insurance agencies and through them onto taxpayers and conservatively managed competitors who knowingly or unknowingly backstop the limited insurance reserves these agencies hold. As long as large deposit institutions and their creditors may count on drawing federal subsidies to extract themselves from what would otherwise be do-or-die situations, the potentially salutary effects of market discipline have little opportunity to make themselves felt.

The Political Dilemma of Reform

Conceived in 1933 as a device for protecting small depositors and bolstering public confidence in financial institutions the subsequent interplay of political forces has assigned federal deposit insurance a far broader bureaucratic mission. It functions today as a system for implicitly guaranteeing the capacity of the deposit institution system to make good on all but a small percentage of its outstanding debt. These implicit guarantees purchase the appearance of stability at the cost of undermining the fear of failure that ordinarily leads an institution's creditors to impose market discipline on its risk-taking activity. They also shift the burden for financing unfavorable outcomes to taxpayers and conservatively managed financial institutions. The result has been a spate of de facto or market-value insolvencies among insured institutions that would be recognized as a national disaster if politicians had to present the bill for underwriting these insolvencies to the body politic.

To reduce the underwriting bill and to restore market discipline, it is necessary to make deposit institution creditors fear failure again. Meaningful deposit insurance reform must reduce the flow of subsidies to deposit institutions. It must endeavor to shift the burden of underwriting catastrophic financial risks from the general taxpayer and surviving institutions back toward risky institutions and their creditors. We may count on political forces to see that Congress develops a set of rules that ease the burdens of transition. But a better deposit insurance system must be one that increases the cost to insured institutions of following subsidy-exploiting strategies of funding, lending, and product line expansion that have seemed very profitable in the past.

Each variety of reform presented in this chapter promises to complicate the jobs of deposit insurance bureaucrats and to hurt deposit institution stockholders and managers to some degree. Nevertheless because they see the need to restore financial stability, most of these parties support deposit insurance reform in principle. But individually they support and oppose different combinations of the six reforms. Industry trade associations must be expected to lobby vigorously against any subset of the six proposals that in the judgment of their membership threatens to hit the firms they represent with disproportionate force. This leaves every one of the six proposals with important enemies and with virtually no important friends.

Each trade association's greatest fears are that its sector of the deposit institution industry will suffer greatly during the transition to a fairer and sounder system and end up regulated more burdensomely than before. Each wants to minimize the extent to which deposit insurance reform could reduce the value of its particular type of depository firm. Inasmuch as each association's membership acknowledges the nation's need for deposit insurance reform, their active resistance to anything but token reform puts them in the position of a banker who decided to consult a psychiatrist about a problem his brother had been causing him and his family. The problem was that his brother had come to believe he was a chicken. His incessant cackling was upsetting everyone in the household and embarrassing them in front of their friends. The psychiatrist assured the banker that he was a leading expert on fixations of this sort and could cure his brother completely in no more than six sessions of therapy. But rather than being pleased by this news, the banker became more agitated than ever. "Hold on," he said. "We just want the cackling stopped. The eggs he lays make a great breakfast."

Deposit institutions are able to harvest eggs from the deposit insurance system only because their deepest layers of risk-bearing are being unintentionally subsidized. As long as this subsidy continues, incentives exist for managers to bet their firm on the future course of interest rates and on the prosperity of specific projects and geographic areas. Some of these bets must lose, and for the losers nationalization looms as an increasingly likely possibility.

Perhaps the greatest irony of financial regulatory reform in the United States is that a necessary condition for its occurrence is virtually a sufficient condition for a program of reform that pays too little attention to long-term problems. Although reform seldom occurs outside an environment of perceived crisis, a crisis atmosphere favors short-sighted solutions. In the midst of a crisis regulators and politicians pay far more attention to the system's immediate difficulties than to its long-run needs. A sympathetic analogy is to consider how hard it would be for a football coach to prepare his team to play its season on dry fields, when fate dictates that their training camp must be held on a quagmire.

Today two immediate difficulties frame the problems that regulators see. First, because authorities have proved reluctant to declare de jure failures in the past, the market value of the nonequity liabilities of most deposit institutions exceeds the market value of the assets that they may recognize under generally accepted accounting principles. Second, because of this, the staffs and explicit insurance reserves of the deposit insurance agencies are overwhelmed. The inadequacy of explicit agency reserves leads agency managers to resort to selling regulatory exemptions and to emphasize noncash forms of assistance such as income-maintenance agreements and ownership positions. At the same time staff limitations permit them to discipline only a few of the many institutions that engage in excessive risk-taking. These constraints make it hard for the average number of de jure failures to exceed two a week, while the pricing of deposit insurance continues to lead insolvent deposit institution managers to pursue a go-for-broke strategy.

It is not necessary for Congress to incorporate all of this chapter's six options into the new-model deposit insurance system. Nor is it necessary that the options finally chosen be installed all at once. Although the complete package probably would produce the best results, adopting any subset of the six options would result in a system that in future years would operate with greater safety, reliability, and comfort. Of course, just how safe, reliable, and comfortable a ride the nation enjoys depends also on the macroeconomic policies that the government follows. If Congress could bring government spending under long-run control, monetary policy would not have to push interest rates over so wide a cycle. Reducing the volatility of interest rates would relieve the car's drivers of the need to take it over quite so dangerous a set of roads.

References and Additional Readings

Benston, George J. 1983. "Deposit Insurance and Bank Failures." *Economic Review*, Federal Reserve Bank of Atlanta (March): 4–17.

Bierwag, G. O., and George G. Kaufman. 1983. "A Proposal for Federal Deposit Insurance with Risk Sensitive Premiums." Occasional paper no. 83-3. Chicago: Federal Reserve Bank of Chicago, March 16.

Campbell, Tim S., and David Glenn. 1984. "Deposit Insurance in a Deregulated Environment." *Journal of Finance* 39 (July): 775–785.

England, Catherine, and John Palffy. 1982. "Replacing the FDIC: Private Insurance for Bank Deposits." *Heritage Foundation Backgrounder*, 229, December 2.

Federal Deposit Insurance Corporation. 1983. *Deposit Insurance in a Changing Environment*. Washington, D.C., April 15.

Federal Home Loan Bank Board. 1983. *Agenda for Reform*. Washington, D.C., March 23.

Horvitz, Paul M. 1975. "Failures of Large Banks: Implications for Deposit Insurance and Banking Supervision." *Journal of Financial and Quantitative Analysis* 10 (November): 589–601.

Horvitz, Paul M. "The Case against Risk-Related Deposit Insurance Premiums." *Housing Finance Review* 2 (July): 253–263.

Kane, Edward J. 1983. "A Six-Point Program for Deposit Insurance Reform." *Housing Finance Review* 2 (July): 269–278.

Kareken, John H. 1983. "Deposit Insurance Reform of Deregulation Is the Cart Not the Horse." *Quarterly Review*, Federal Reserve Bank of Minneapolis (Spring): 1–9.

Kramer, Orin S. 1984. "Putting More Pain into Bank Failures." *Fortune*, February 20, pp. 135–142.

Maisel, Sherman J., ed. 1981. *Risk and Capital Adequacy in Commercial Banks*. Chicago: University of Chicago Press and the National Bureau of Economic Research.

Mayer, Thomas A. 1975. "Should Large Banks Be Allowed to Fail?" *Journal of Financial and Quantitative Analysis* 10 (November): 603–613.

Pyle, David H. 1983. "Pricing Deposit Insurance: The Effects of Mismeasurement." Unpublished working paper. Federal Reserve Bank of San Francisco and School of Business Administration, University of California, Berkeley, October.

Pyle, David H. 1984. "Deregulation and Deposit Insurance Reform." *Economic Review*, Federal Reserve Bank of San Francisco (Spring): 5–15.

Short, Eugenie D., and Gerald P. O'Driscoll, Jr. 1983. "Deregulation and Deposit Insurance." *Economic Review*, Federal Reserve Bank of Dallas (September): 11–22.

Index

Accord, 80
Accounting gimmicks, 81
Accounting principles, 89, 90, 133, 145, 148, 165. *See also* Book value accounting; Market value accounting
 deferred accounting, 81, 116
 intrinsic-value accounting, 20, 148
 purchase accounting, 43, 56
 regulatory accounting, 20, 43, 148
Accounting profits, 93, 94, 107, 116, 125, 151
Accounting write-downs, 20, 75, 89, 90, 116, 125–128
 mandatory date, 127
Acquisitions, 43–45, 70–72, 143. *See also* Takeovers
Actuarial value, 47, 48, 52, 66, 84, 143
Adam Smith ties, 122
Adaptive efficiency, 160
Adjustable rate mortgages, 110
Administrative discipline, 6, 7, 17, 19, 21, 48, 60, 82, 87, 122, 154
Administrative forbearance, 21
Adverse selection, 60, 62, 64, 112, 146, 158
Aetna, 160
Affiliated institution risk, 8, 9, 14, 47, 62, 63, 81, 134
Agencies' five-point rating scale, 153
Aharoni, Yair, 57
ALCO, 80, 111, 112, 156
Altman, Edward I., 134, 144
American City Bank, 46, 69
Antitrust exemptions, 6, 45, 56
Appraisal techniques, 150
Arbitrage, 14, 87, 113
Argentina, 75, 126, 161
Aspinwall, Richard C., 28
Assessment income, 50, 67, 75, 112
Asset and liability powers, 114
Asset-liability committee. *See* ALCO
Asset-liability mismatching, 8, 12, 17, 21, 22, 65, 93–95, 103, 111, 112

Asset quality, 133
Assistance, 21, 35, 39, 40, 42, 50, 52, 54–56, 70–71, 76, 124, 143, 162
 packages, 51
 policy innovations, 50, 53–57
 noncash forms, 165
Assisted mergers, 51, 76
 mutual savings banks, 51
Assumability options, 110
Asymmetries due to size, 48, 49, 67
Automated teller machines, 64
Automobile-insurance metaphor, 87
Automotive metaphor, 1, 3, 4, 146–148, 165
Average life of assets, 93–95

Bad debt reserves, 110
Bailouts, 5, 25, 26, 34, 60, 143, 145, 162
Balance of payments, 127
Balance sheet
 augmented, 45, 133
 conventional, 48, 56
 deterioration, 48, 133
 identity, 107
Bank of America, 44
Bank discount basis, 78
Bank holding companies, 8, 9, 12, 17, 20, 31, 32, 47, 49, 62, 63, 64, 76, 81, 134, 158
 parent, 63, 64, 155, 158
 subsidiaries, 32, 45, 63
Bank of International Settlements, 74, 126
Bankruptcy, 5, 38, 49, 81
Bank stock prices, 126, 127, 149
Barnett, Robert E., 38, 57, 76, 84
Batlin, Carl, 110, 117
Beesley, H. Brent, 55
Below-market Fed loans, 5, 37, 49
Benston, George J., 28, 84, 120, 144, 160, 166
Betting the firm, 14, 159, 164
Bierwag, G. O., 166

Bilateral interbank credit limits, 140
Bill for underwriting insolvencies, 1, 163
Black, Fisher, 33, 57
Black Sox Scandal, 2
Bomb metaphor, 88–89
Bookable assets, 42, 43
Bookable net worth, 11, 106, 116
Book entry security, 66
Book value, 36, 46, 76, 81, 89, 90, 91, 92, 93, 101, 102, 105, 116, 121, 125, 135, 136, 137, 148, 150, 151
Book value accounting, 12, 25, 119, 149
Book value insolvency, 35, 36
Boyd, John H., 84
Branch banking, 19, 64
Braniff, 128
Brazil, 75, 126, 161
Brickley, James, 103, 117
Brokerage activities, 17
Brokered deposits, 34, 79, 80, 120, 131, 132, 156
amount, 132, 133
Brooks, Thomas A., 41, 54, 55, 57
Building inspectors parable, 146
Bunching. *See* Risk
Burden of adjustment, 22, 60, 163, 164
Burdens of regulation, 32, 164
shifting, 14, 32, 60
Bureaucratic breakdown, 1, 13, 27, 143, 147, 152, 154
Bureaucratic incentives, 6, 7, 11, 19, 26, 32, 39, 52, 60, 79, 82, 87, 123–124, 154, 161, 162, 163
Bureaucratic interests, 21, 36
Burns, Helen M., 18, 28
Buser, Stephen A., 23, 28, 82, 84, 117
Business cycle, 21, 23, 33, 59
Business failures, 61

Call reports, 15, 80, 99
Cancellation rights, 25, 151–156
Campbell, Tim S., 166
Capital, 15, 20, 21, 23, 36, 37, 40, 60, 62, 63, 64, 76, 79, 81, 94, 103, 116, 125, 135, 141
account (*see* Equity; Net worth)
adequacy, 77, 79, 81, 82, 96, 116
primary, 138
requirements, 63, 67, 79, 82, 149, 151, 153

Capitalized value, 97, 103, 106, 115. *See also* Present discounted value
Capital losses, 89, 90, 98
Capital riddle, 141–142
Caps on nominal interest rates, 128
Career risk as counterincentive, 113, 115, 123, 161
Cash management account, 160
Cash market for LDC loans, 124
CD, 36, 77, 97, 107–109, 115, 128, 129, 130
CD brokerage, 80, 131, 132, 152, 155, 158. *See also* Brokered deposits
CD rate, 78, 109
CD risk premium, 77–79
CDx, 132
Cease and desist orders, 48, 153, 154
Central bank, 22, 33
Certificate of deposit. *See* CD
Charter, 105, 106, 119, 152
value, 36, 82
Charter conversions, 113, 115
Chartering authority, 20, 21, 33, 36, 152. *See also* Supervision
Chen, Andrew H., 23, 28, 82, 84, 117
Chicken parable, 164
Chrysler, 128
Cigna Corporation, 160
Citicorp, 160
Citizens & Southern National Bank, 44
Claims settlement, 80, 81
Clean assets, 45
Clean-bank transactions, 43
Clearing, 133, 139–140
Clearinghouse associations, 139–140
Clearing House Interbank Payment System (CHIPS), 140
Closed-bank transactions, 41, 47, 48
Closing. *See* Failure
Coinsurance, 83, 158
Collateral rights, 38, 98
Collection problems, 52, 65, 139, 140
Commonwealth Savings Company, 5
Compliance costs, 81
Confidence, 11, 13, 15, 22, 33, 39, 77, 100, 142, 161, 163
Congress, 4, 27, 65, 83, 88, 117, 130, 133, 142, 144, 154, 155, 161
banking committees, 24
concurrent resolution, 4, 32, 60, 75, 142

Congressional denial, 26
Conjectural guarantees, 46, 47, 81, 115, 142, 148, 154, 162. *See also* Guarantees, implicit
Conover, Todd, 161
Conservatively managed deposit institutions' interests, 19, 142, 145, 151, 162, 163
Conservatorship, 56
Consolidation of FDIC and FSLIC, 24, 75–76
Constraints on government assistance, 26, 162–163
Continental Illinois Bank and Trust Company, 6, 12, 49, 52, 56, 64, 67, 69, 95, 103, 155
Contingent commitments, 19, 134, 135
Contingent contract writing, 42, 72, 159
Contribution agreements, 56, 70–71. *See also* Assistance
Correspondent banks, 36, 139
Cosmetic accounting, 12, 16, 124, 125, 150
Cost-of-funds index, 54
Country-doctor parable, 26–27, 117
Country risk, 16, 62–65, 156
Covenants, 64
Coverages, 11, 23, 24, 34, 62, 80, 111–112, 122, 141, 146, 152, 156, 157, 160
  basic coverage, 25
  changes over time, 34
  cumulative lifetime limits, 158
  de jure, 131, 155
  limitations, 10, 49, 66, 108, 124, 130, 131
  supplementary, 25, 157–158, 160
Creative FSLIC and FDIC financing, 142
Credibility of guarantee, 23, 31, 35, 59, 106, 156
Credit allocation, 159
Credit crunches, 107, 108
Credit risk, 8, 9, 16, 19, 62
Crisis policies, 162, 165. *See also* Bureaucratic breakdown
Cross-industry acquisitions, 43–46, 143
Customer relationships, 38

Damage control recordkeeping, 12
Dead-bank transaction, 38, 155

Debt restructurings, 17, 121, 122, 125, 127, 128
  involuntary concessions, 75
Debt service, 130
Deductibles, 83, 158
De facto guarantees. *See* Conjectural guarantees
De facto or market-value insolvencies, 10, 11, 13, 18, 20, 39, 60, 66, 148, 152, 162–163. *See also* Insolvency
Default, 2, 21, 22, 75, 90
Default risk, 4, 20
Department of Housing and Urban Development, 105, 118
Deposit assumptions, 72, 76
Deposit insurance
  bank, 40
  beneficiary interests, 1, 33, 130
  contract design, 83, 141, 147, 160
  costs, 3–5, 17, 46, 49, 50, 53, 83, 96, 112, 158
  crisis, 4, 6, 27 (*see also* Bureaucratic breakdown)
  goals and purpose, 32, 33, 37, 66, 163
  guarantees, 13, 23, 96, 107 (*see also* Guarantees)
  legislative history, 18
  mandatory enrollment, 34
  of nondepository institution, 120, 128–129
  pricing, 13, 18, 19, 24, 57, 80, 82, 87, 106, 110, 112, 114–116, 122, 143–144, 146, 149, 157, 158, 160 (*see also* Insurance premiums)
  problems, 18
  reform, 24, 26, 27, 97, 143, 144, 145–165
  reserves or fund, 4, 6, 14, 44, 46, 47, 50, 52, 56, 60, 67, 70–71, 75–77, 97, 100, 112, 142, 155, 162, 165
  settlement actions, 70–71
  standards board, 159
  structural weaknesses, 59, 62
  subcontracting, 128–129
  subsidy (*see* Subsidy to risk-bearing)
  taxpayer interests in, 1, 11, 146
  termination, 11, 21, 25, 152, 154
Deposit payoffs, 38, 39, 45, 47, 51, 52, 56, 113, 135
Deposit rate regulation, 64, 95, 106, 107, 115

Deposit transfer, 41, 46, 154
Depositor withdrawal options, 22, 97
Depository Institutions Deregulation Committee, 115
Depository Institutions Deregulation and Monetary Control Act of 1980, 76, 114
Deregulation, 12, 17, 114, 115
Dilemma of reform, 13, 163–164
Dirty assets, 45
Disclosure, 12, 16, 17, 25, 48, 135, 150, 151
Discounted present value, 66, 94, 97, 103, 106, 150. *See also* Capitalized value
Discount window. *See* Lender of last resort
Disintermediation, 108
Distributional effects, 17, 18, 32–33, 35, 60, 83, 112, 115, 116, 131, 142, 143, 146, 147, 158
Diversifiability of insurance risk, 59
Diversification, 8, 62, 114, 115
Divisibility, 157
Double leveraging, 63
Due-on-sale clause, 105
Dun and Bradstreet, 61
Duration, 93, 94, 110–111

Economic efficiency, 18, 20, 32, 33, 60, 143
Economic interest of insurers, 32–33
Eisenbeis, Robert, 84
Embezzlement, 16
Emergency treatment, 5, 37, 123, 124
Emerging risks, 13, 19, 25, 83, 119–144, 161
Emerson, Guy, 18, 28
Endgame plays, 132, 152, 155
Enforcement actions, 17, 83, 153
England, Catherine, 166
Entry regulation, 106
Equity, 15, 21, 23, 39, 49, 63, 65, 77, 83, 84, 107, 119, 143, 159
  data on bank equity, 137–138
Examinations, 7, 15, 16, 17, 19, 20, 24, 26, 33, 36, 82, 83, 133, 135, 151, 155, 156
Examiner incentives, 144
Exclusion clauses, 83

Executive separation contracts, 38, 113
Explicit claims, 110, 119
Explicit interest rates, 25, 95
Explicit premiums. *See* Insurance premiums
Explicit pricing, 14, 82, 143, 144
Ex post settlement, 158–159
Extended liability for stockholders, 158

Face value, 104
Failing-rate exposure, 94, 96. *See also* Asset-liability mismatching
Failure, 1, 7, 10, 14, 16, 18–25, 34, 37–38, 41, 45–46, 50, 52–53, 66–67, 79, 82, 113, 148, 158, 161, 163
  cost minimization, 45–47
  de jure, 37, 149, 162, 165
  largest ones, 69
  major causes, 10, 20, 81
  prevention, 7, 11
  rate, 2, 18, 61, 81
  resolution, 11, 42, 46, 122 (*see also* Insolvency resolution)
  spread, 10, 33, 37
Fair pricing, 52, 117, 146
Federal Financial Institutions Examination Council, 12, 15, 33, 79, 80
Federal funds, 95, 161
Federal guarantees, 19, 107, 130, 161–162
Federal Housing Administration, 105, 118
FHLB advances, 79, 106
FHLBB survey data, 108
Fiduciary responsibilities, 32
Financial analysts, 65, 149
Financial Institution and Interest Rate Control Act of 1978, 15
Financial Institution Assurance Corporation, 154
Financial services, 62, 120, 134
Financial structure, 25, 34
First Tennessee National Corp., 44
Fiscal policy, 127, 165
Fixed-rate instruments, 93, 95, 105
Flannery, Mark J., 117
Flechsig, Theodore G., 24, 29, 48, 58
Football team analogy, 165
Foreclosure rights, 19
Foreign exchange risk, 8, 9, 16, 36, 139

Foreign lending, 12, 72–75, 115, 119, 150
Forward and futures transactions, 34, 36, 96, 111–114, 134, 139
Fragility of system, 1, 3, 146, 163
Franklin National Bank, 38, 69
Fraud, 81
Fresh yields, 93, 94
Funding, 81, 158, 163
Furash, Edward E., 134, 144
Futures transactions. *See* Forward and futures transactions

Gaps. *See* Asset-liability mismatches
Garn-St Germain Institutions Act of 1982, 31, 39–40, 44, 114
Gay, Gerald D., 118
Geographic span of operations, 14, 67, 114
Geological metaphor, 59
Gibson, William E., 24, 28
Glenn, David, 166
GNMA, 114
"Go-for-broke mode," 107
Going concern, 38, 41
Goldberg, Ellen S., 134, 135, 144
Goldberg, Michael A., 136, 144
Golembe, Carter H., 18, 28
Golodner, Pat, 51
Goodwill, 42, 43, 81, 106
Gough, Robert P., 61
Gould, Julia A., 71, 84
Government's equity stake, 23, 40, 56–57. *See also* Insurer's equity stake
Grandfathering, 34
Green, George D., 18, 28
Greenwich Savings Bank, 51, 53
Guarantees, 23, 31, 32–33, 34, 45, 49, 59, 65, 66, 72, 96, 98, 102, 105, 106, 116, 131, 135, 139, 145
  explicit, 96–97, 142
  implicit, 13, 47, 75, 76, 97, 108, 148, 163 (*see also* Conjectural guarantees)
  market value, 1, 6, 66, 84, 96, 103, 106, 146, 156
  participations, 135
  underpricing, 13, 23, 57, 113, 116, 132
Guttentag, Jack, 6, 28, 107, 117

Hangover of low-interest-rate mortgages, 3, 97–110

Hanweck, Gerald, 120, 138, 144
Hedging, 94, 111–112
Herring, Richard, 107, 117
Hobson, Ronald B., 114, 117
Hoenig, Thomas, 16, 29
Holding company. *See* Bank holding companies
Hopewell, M. H., 93, 117
Horvitz, Paul M., 28, 38, 57, 76, 84, 159, 166
Hoy, Michael, 83, 84
Humphrey, David B., 28, 120, 144
Hyperactive regulation, 87

Implicit claims, 63, 64, 110, 119
Implicit interest, 64
Implicit premiums. *See* Administrative discipline; Insurance premiums; Regulatory sanctions
Implicit pricing, 14, 82, 143
Implicit values, 56, 107, 119
Incentive-compatible insurance contracts, 83, 146
Income-maintenance agreements, 42, 45, 51, 53, 54, 56, 165
  recapture provisions, 54
Income tax payments by deposit institutions, 99, 100
Indemnification, 38, 41, 43, 45, 56
Indexed coverage, 157
Indirect payoff, 41
Industrial and development bonds, 130
Industry risk, 156
Inequitable distribution of net premiums. *See* Distributional effects
Inflation, 126, 128
Informational asymmetry, 7, 32, 33, 60, 62, 65, 146, 148, 156
Information risk, 151
Information system, 11, 27, 80, 111, 151, 154, 156, 157, 159. *See also* Reporting system
Innovation. *See* Emerging risks
Insolvency, 2, 10, 13, 20, 26, 34, 37, 39, 67, 133, 135, 139, 148, 151, 155, 165. *See also* De facto or market-value insolvencies
  de jure, 10, 11, 20, 148
Insolvency resolution policies, 11, 13, 41, 31–58, 70–71, 98, 133, 153, 161, 162

Insolvency resolution policies (cont.)
  costs and benefits, 3, 5, 33–34, 38, 45, 46, 49, 51, 60, 70–72
  myopia in, 33–34, 60
Insurance. *See* Deposit insurance
Insurance premiums, 52, 57, 62, 66, 67, 72, 77, 80, 144, 160
  ex ante vs. ex post, 158–160
  explicit, 19, 24, 32, 34, 67, 81–83, 87, 112, 139, 141, 145, 146, 158, 161
  graduated, 24, 26
  implicit, 19, 24, 81, 83, 87, 97, 112 (*see also* Administrative discipline; regulatory sanctions)
  mandated rebate level, 67
  rebates, 52, 67, 76
Insurance subsidies. *See* Subsidy to risk-bearing
Insurer equity stake, 11, 23, 49, 66, 77
Insurer insolvency, 19, 59
Interagency competition, 25, 33, 34, 148, 152–154, 160–161
  span of regulatory control, 66
  specialized regulators, 17, 114
Interbank payments risk, 133, 139–140
Interest ceilings. *See* Deposit rate regulation
Interest group politics, 31, 32, 107, 154, 163–164
  trade associations, 81, 164
Interest rate bet. *See* Interest volatility risk
Interest rate risk. *See* Interest volatility risk
Interest sensitivity, 89, 107, 108, 150. *See also* Asset-liability mismatching
Interest volatility, 7, 21, 22, 23, 53, 64, 66, 79, 80, 103, 165
Interest volatility risk, 4, 8, 9, 19, 22, 42, 52, 57, 62, 64, 65, 77, 80, 82–84, 87–89, 93, 96, 110, 111, 112, 113, 116, 147, 156
Interinstitutional mergers. *See* Cross-industry acquisitions
Internal integrity risk, 8, 9
International Banking Act of 1978, 75
International Lending Act of 1983, 63
International Monetary Fund (IMF), 63, 75, 125
Interstate banking, 20, 43, 45, 132, 143
Interstate takeovers, 43–45, 70–71, 143
Intraday overdrafts, 133, 139–140
Isaac, William, 24, 61

Jaffe, Naomi L., 114, 117
James, Christopher, 103, 117
Jumbo CDs, 108, 109, 115

Kane, Edward J., 23, 28, 82, 84, 117, 144, 148, 166
Kareken, John, 28, 166
Kaufman, George C., 93, 117, 118, 166
Klebaner, Benjamin J., 20, 28
Kolb, Robert W., 118
Kramer, Orin S., 166
Kreps, Clifton, 28

LaGesse, David, 81
Large denomination deposits, 76, 78, 108
Latin American debt, 122, 125, 126
Law of one price, 112
LDC debt, 73, 120–126, 128, 146, 150
Leff, Gary, 28
Lender of last resort, 22, 37, 59, 141, 142, 162–163
Leverage, 21, 63, 64, 105, 113, 147
Leverage risk, 4, 163
Limited liability, 105, 158
Lines of credit, 35, 75, 107
Linked financing, 128–130
Liquidation, 6, 11, 38, 41, 42, 45, 46, 49, 50, 52, 76, 113, 144, 150, 155
  reluctance to liquidate a large institution, 161
Liquidity risk, 8, 9, 19, 157
Liquidity shortages, 17, 35, 66
Live-bank acquisition, 38
Lloyd-Davies, Peter R., 135, 136, 144
Loan offsets. *See* Rights of offset
Loan restructurings. *See* Debt restructurings
Long-funding, 83, 94, 96, 111. *See also* Asset-liability mismatching
Long position, 14, 114

McCarthy, Edward J., 109
McCulloch, J. Huston, 24, 28, 52, 57, 65, 84, 103, 118
Macroeconomic policy risk, 22, 128. *See also* Interest volatility

Maisel, Sherman J., 28, 84, 144, 166
Malfeasance, 36
Mallison, Eugenie, 95, 118
Mann, John, 85
Marcus, Alan J., 52, 57, 103, 118
Market discipline, 4, 11, 17, 25, 141, 146, 149, 157, 161, 162, 163
Market failure, 121–122
Market value, 12, 36, 46, 70–71, 80, 90, 104, 105, 107, 124, 125, 126, 127, 149, 150, 152, 165
Market value accounting, 12, 25, 75, 124, 148, 151
Market value insolvencies. *See* De facto insolvencies
Market value of S&L and MSB net worth accounts, 76–77, 101–102
Market value of a firm's stock, 8, 12, 36, 107
Marking to market, 89
Marvell, Thomas, 57
Match funding, 80, 94, 110, 111, 115
Maturity, 65, 79, 80, 97, 104, 105, 110
Mayer, Thomas, 24, 29, 166
Mayers, David P., 14, 29, 62, 83, 85
Meigs, A. James, 122, 144
Merger, 37, 42, 52, 67, 70–71, 106
Merger assistance. *See* Assistance
Merrill Lynch, 132, 160
Merton, Robert C., 24, 29, 57
Mexico, 75, 122, 126, 127, 161
Miller, Merton, 33, 52, 57
Miller, Randall J., 58, 118
Minority stockholders, 12
Mismatches. *See* Asset-liability mismatching
Models, 42, 80, 102, 103, 106
Modified payoff, 155
Monetary policy, 21, 33, 79, 80, 93, 127
Money-creating power, 5, 59, 60
Money market mutual funds, 130, 157
Monitoring, 33, 67, 80, 81, 145, 152–154
Moral hazard, 14, 15, 62, 87
Morgan Guaranty Trust, 122
Mortgage interest rates, 90–93, 105
Mortgage life expectancy, 105
Mortgagor options, 110

National Credit Union Administration, 15

National Credit Union Share Insurance Fund, 31
Nationalization, 5, 6, 13, 39, 49, 52, 143, 164, 165
  de facto, 40, 56, 57, 84, 165
  denationalization, 6, 65
Nebraska Depository Institutions Guaranty Corporation, 4
Net worth, 2, 20, 22, 43, 65, 76, 77, 79, 81, 96, 98, 101, 102, 103, 105, 116, 119, 125, 139, 140, 152, 162
Net worth certificates, 40, 81, 142
New York Bank for Savings, 53
Nondeposit liabilities, 36, 41, 47, 105
Nondepository financial services firms, 24–25, 63
Nonequity liabilities, 107, 165
Nonperforming loans, 12, 17, 81, 104, 127
Nontraditional forms of risk. *See* Emerging risks
Nontrusteed deferred compensation plans, 130

O'Driscoll, Gerald P., Jr., 166
Off-balance-sheet items, 105, 120, 133
OPEC, 73
Open-bank takeover, 41, 47, 48
Operating efficiency risk, 8, 9
Opportunity costs, 46, 53, 89, 98, 105
Option pricing, 42, 53
Options transactions, 53, 96, 110, 111, 112
Organization for Economic Cooperation and Development, 126
Overregulation of recognized risks, 88, 119

Palffy, John, 166
Paper gains. *See* Unrealized gains and losses
Parables
  chicken, 164
  country-doctor, 26–27, 117
  skyscraper inspection trip, 122–124
Parent. *See* Bankholding companies
Park, J. W., 28
Par valuation, 126, 127
Past due loans. *See* Nonperforming loans
Paydown assumptions, 53

Payments moratoria, 128
Penn Square Bank, 43, 52, 69, 135
Perry, Philip R., 29
Perverse incentives, 11, 13, 14, 19, 34, 50, 64, 65, 82, 107, 117, 146
  for mutual institutions, 113
Philippines, 161
Phoenix institution, 5–6, 40, 56, 57
Pierce, James, 28
Pithyachariyakul, Pipat, 84
Poland, 75
Political constituencies. *See* Interest group politics
Political incentives, 2, 7, 10, 13, 19, 26, 32, 39, 52, 62, 65, 75, 81, 107, 112, 117, 127, 142, 145, 160–165
Politically protected risks, 121, 122, 143, 145, 150
Ponzi scheme, 159
Portfolio risk, 8, 26, 115, 116
Posner, Richard, 33, 57
Precautionary balances, 157
Premium structure, 66, 80, 156
Prepayment options, 105, 110
Present value. *See* Discounted present value
Price of risk-bearing services, 14, 113, 159
Private deposit insurance, 24, 25, 37, 59, 65, 148, 160–161, 162
Problem institutions, 2, 16, 20, 59, 61, 70–71, 72, 77, 152
Product line, 14, 63, 67, 114, 163
Proxmire, William, 35
Pseudo-default rate, 90, 91, 92, 93, 98, 101, 102, 104
  estimation bias in, 104
Pseudo-reserves, 142
Public confidence. *See* Confidence
Purchase-and-assumption transactions, 39, 41, 42, 43, 45, 46, 47, 48, 98
Purchase premium, 42
Put options, 96
Pyle, David H., 118, 159, 166

Reagan, Ronald, 12
Realization of gains and losses, 52, 90
Real or inflation-adjusted rate of interest, 80, 120, 121, 122, 128
Rebates of assessment income. *See* Insurance premiums

Receivership, 41
Recycling of petrodollars, 73
Regulator-arranged auctions, 150
Regulatory distortions. *See* Perverse incentives
Regulatory exemptions, 44, 45, 50, 56, 143, 165
Regulatory interference. *See* Administrative discipline; Implicit premiums
Regulatory lags, 19, 60, 65, 77, 87, 120, 140, 143, 145
Regulatory risk, 8, 9, 62
Regulatory sanctions. *See* Administrative discipline; Implicit premiums
Regulatory strategy, 114
Regulatory structure, 122
Reinsurance, 24, 25, 160, 161
Reorganization of troubled firms, 39, 40
Repayment problems, 65, 120, 121, 124, 127, 141
Reporting system, 80, 81, 111, 156
  asymmetries between FDIC and FSLIC, 72
  electronic reporting, 81, 156
Repurchase agreements, 34, 36, 108, 115
Reserve ratios. *See* Deposit insurance, reserves or fund
Revell, J. R. S., 140, 144
Rights of offset, 38, 98
Rising-rate exposure, 94, 96
Risk, 8, 10, 16, 21, 25, 59, 82, 89, 139, 145
  bunching, 10, 59, 62, 66
  exotic forms, 159
  shifting, 13, 32, 62, 65, 67, 84, 95
  sources, 8
  unregulated, 20, 21, 63–64, 82, 88, 97, 112, 113, 116, 120, 143, 145, 149
Risk classes, 83, 144
Risk exposure, 72, 80, 87, 95, 100, 112, 139, 149, 158, 159, 160
  to changing interest rates, 94, 96
Risk management, 7, 10, 11, 26, 72, 80, 83, 87, 88, 112, 151
Risk measurement, 26, 79, 112, 159
Risk of failure, 1, 14, 21, 81
Risk premiums, 78, 96, 97, 107, 108
Risk-rated premiums, 18, 19, 24, 82, 112, 115, 116, 149, 157, 158, 160. *See also* Insurance premiums

Risk-sensitive pricing. *See* Risk-rated premiums
Risk signalling, 157
Risks of obsolescence, 10, 64
Risk-taking
  categories, 62
  incentives (*see* Perverse incentives)
  strategies, 62, 149, 163
  voluntary, 8, 11, 27, 62, 146, 165
Rollover, 36
Rosenberg, Barr, 29
Rothschild, Michael, 83, 85
Runs, 35, 36, 50, 127, 148
  systemic, 5, 60, 142, 162

Safety and soundness, 7, 32, 37, 48, 67, 141, 153
S and L phoenix institutions. *See* Phoenix institution
Scholl, Russ, 73
Scott, Kenneth W., 24, 29
Seafirst Corporation, 44
Seasoned mortgages, 90, 93, 105
Seaway National Bank, 46
Secondary markets, 150
Securities and Exchange Commission (SEC), 12, 16, 17, 150
Securities Investor Protection Corporation, 160
Service facility risk, 8, 19
Settlement, 133, 139, 140
Shaked, Israel, 52, 57, 103, 118
Shoeless Joe Jackson, 2
Short, Eugenie D., 166
Short funding, 19, 56, 83, 90, 94, 95, 96, 110, 111. *See also* Asset-liability mismatching
Short position, 14, 95
Silverberg, Stanley C., 24, 29, 38, 48, 51, 57, 58, 76, 84
Simple interest basis, 78
Sinkey, Joseph F., 8, 10, 16, 29, 61, 81, 85, 134, 144
Smith, Clifford L., Jr., 14, 29, 62, 83, 85
Soundness. *See* Safety and soundness
Sovereign risk, 72, 73, 82, 83, 88. *See also* Country risk
Speculation, 83, 114, 116, 164
Spong, Kenneth, 16, 29
Spooking uninsured depositors, 48

Stability, 3, 33, 161, 162, 163, 164. *See also* Fragility of system
Standby commitments. *See* Contingent commitments
Standby letters of credit (SLC), 133–136, 139
  data, 136
State-chartered institutions, 33, 34
State insurance systems, 18
Stiglitz, Joseph, 83, 85
Stigum, Marcia, 78, 85
Stockholder interests, 12, 25, 39, 41, 113, 115, 121, 135–136, 146, 148, 158, 163
Straddle, 96
Subcontracting guarantees, 132, 139
Subordination arrangements, 41, 42, 45
Subsidiaries. *See* Bank holding companies
Subsidies, 5, 18, 32, 37, 49, 51, 53, 120, 127, 141, 158
  lending to LDCs, 121–128
Subsidy shifting, 117, 119, 120, 122, 132
Subsidy to risk-bearing, 25, 26, 32, 82, 83, 95, 113, 115, 117, 119, 122, 145, 146, 157, 163
  unintended, 132, 164
Substitution of government equity for private capital. *See* Government's equity stake
Supervision, 15, 25, 33, 82. *See also* Examination; Monitoring
Supervisory actions, 20, 24, 44, 48, 113
Supervisory authority, 20, 152–154. *See also* Chartering authority
Supplemental assessments, 75
Surveillance. *See* Supervision
Swaps, 125

Takeover bidding, 6, 57
  constraints on eligible bidders, 44, 46
Takeovers, 42
  voluntary *vs.* involuntary, 20, 42
Talley, Samuel H., 136, 144
Taxpayer interests, 1, 142, 144, 145, 147, 153, 162, 163
Tax write-off capacity, 38, 90, 98, 108, 110, 116
Technical insolvency. *See* Book value insolvency

Technological risk, 8, 9, 16, 62, 64, 82, 83, 88
Theft, 16, 20, 36
Timme, Stephen G., 118
Transactional efficiency, 14, 132, 157
Transitional burdens. *See* Burdens of adjustment
Triage. *See* Emergency treatment
Treasury bill rate, 22–23, 78, 108, 109
Troubled loans, 141, 150. *See also* Nonperforming loans
Truncation of losses by guarantees, 34, 105
Trusteed arrangements, 130, 155
Tulsa (Oklahoma) County Home Finance Authority, 128

Ultimate guarantors. *See* Taxpayer interests
Ulysses, 161
Unaccounted income flows, 52, 100, 162
Unbookable values, 42, 43, 49, 56, 106
Unbooked values, 37, 97, 98, 101, 102, 104, 105, 106, 107, 116
Understatement of FDIC losses, 52, 53
Underwater claims, 49, 107, 121, 124, 125, 145
Undisclosed values, 38, 45, 56
Undocumented claims, 43
Unfavorable publicity. *See* Disclosure
Unfunded guarantees, 13, 32, 142, 146, 159
Uninsured creditors, 3, 19, 36, 37, 38, 98, 142
Uninsured depositors, 25, 45, 48, 107, 131, 133, 147–148
Uninsured deposits, 34, 35, 38, 39, 40, 155
Uninsured liabilities, 35, 39, 41, 42, 45, 76, 77, 96, 107, 108, 115
Union Dime Savings Bank, 51, 53
Union National Bank of Chicago, 46
United American Bank of Knoxville, 44, 69
United States National Bank, 69
Unrealized gains and losses, 20, 36, 76, 90, 100, 104, 105, 150, 162
U.S. Treasury, 26, 38, 80, 98, 130, 157

Variable-rate loans, 104, 116

Vartanian, Thomas P., 41, 54, 55, 57
Venezuela, 126, 161
Volcker, Paul, 121

Wacht, R. F., 28
Wallace, Neil, 28
Washington Federal Savings and Loan Association of University Heights, Ohio, 114
World Bank, 75
Write-down. *See* Accounting write-down

Yield curve, 111